Behavior Management Skills Guide

Practical Activities & Interventions For Ages 3-18

Proven and Effective Tools

Disruptive Behavior I ADHD I Anxiety I Asperger's I ODD
Non-Compliance I Mood Disorders I Developmental Delays

Scott Walls, MA, LIPC, CCMHC & Deb Rauner, M.Ed

Published by
PESI Publishing & Media
PESI, Inc
3839 White Ave
Eau Claire, WI 54703

Cover: Amy Rubenzer
Editing: Blair Davis
Layout: Bookmasters

ISBN: 9781937661663

Printed in the United States of America

PESI
Publishing
& Media
www.pesipublishing.com

Table of Contents

Section I

GETTING ORIENTED

CHAPTER 1

Introduction & How To Use This Book

Our time spent working with kids in multiple settings has led us to some mutual, foundational beliefs about what we do in this work. The underlying notion and something that you, the reader, will likely note as you read through this guide is that there needs to be a foundation of success. Essentially, the idea is that when working with kids, we need to set the stage for success early on.

By setting the stage for success, programming and even behavior modification become easier and actually healthier for all involved. Because we have written this guide for all readers, we fully expect that the intention of those using this book is to **increase positive behaviors** while decreasing negative behaviors. Much of what you will learn in this book is how to set up kids in a good way so that everyone benefits.

Working with kids with challenging behaviors is actually challenging! Without having strategies and techniques that lend to positive interactions and results, working with challenging behaviors can lead to frustration at a minimum and even total burnout and fatigue.

Reinforcement is another essential piece of what we intend to teach and is the foundation of most human behavior. Even in terms of survival, as humans we move toward what is most reinforcing to us. In terms of non-survival behavior, we often seek out whatever reinforcement we can find, even if it is not good for us. Our intention here is to use reinforcement as a driving force to help change challenging behaviors and move toward an overall approach that decreases negative behaviors in kids, increases safety and is easily systematized by the provider.

Even with the very best programming and proactive strategies in place, reacting to behavior is a necessary step in most cases, and this is especially true with more severe behaviors. Again, we **build from a place of success, not failure**, and look at what is reinforcing to that particular kid in that moment. However, we also realize that providers need to know what to do when certain behaviors occur, and we provide clear strategies regarding these situations.

You will find that the strategies and ideas presented are pertinent to many areas of disability including ADHD, Autism, Asperger's Syndrome, Oppositional Defiant Disorder, Mood Disorders as well as for individuals with Developmental Delays. Specific strategies should be utilized based on an individual's needs, not based on the disability area.

For example, we have found in our experience, that presenting proactive and reactive strategies in a visual format is beneficial not only to individuals on the Autism Spectrum but for many students who are experiencing behavioral difficulties in general. Many of our examples and ideas are presented using a visual format that will be applicable to many.

In this book, when you read the word *provider,* we are speaking of the adult in charge. This might be an educator, therapist, parent, daycare provider, doctor, nurse, teacher, classroom assistant, principal or other adult. When we say *child, kid, youth*, etc., we are talking about a person at or around the age of the group targeted in each section of the guide (e.g., pre-school–age child, middle school–age child). We use alternating gender pronouns throughout.

This book has many lists and handouts that you are free to use. We like books and manuals from which we are able to extract information and then put that information into action. So, our book is designed to do that while giving you the material you need to allow these programming ideas to be easily used.

We understand that behavior management run across all economic, cultural, racial and gender populations. We also realize that what is important for one subgroup of a population can be much different than what is needed for another subgroup. If a kid is worried about his next meal or about where he is going to stay the next night, he has a much different problem than the kid who is upset about not getting to play her video game that night. We make every attempt to be sensitive to different groups and encourage you to adjust the material to individual situations as appropriate and as needed.

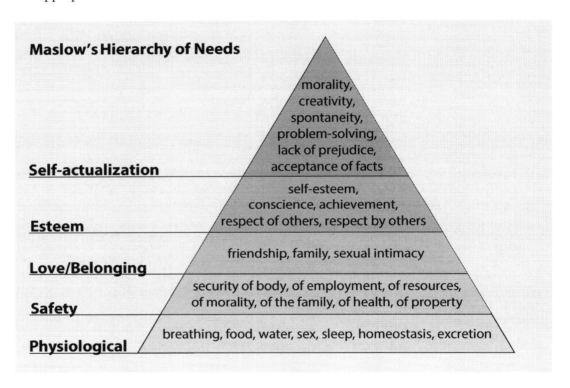

Maslow's Hierarchy of Needs

We believe that in moving toward self-esteem and self-actualization, one needs to be able to behave in multiple environments. Simply put, kids who are getting in trouble and exhibiting outrageous behaviors have difficulty moving past the Safety and Love/Belonging stages and can often get stuck. We want to help you use positive behavior management to help kids move up the hierarchy of needs toward their full potential.

Using this book is simple. One does not have to read it from cover to cover; rather, you may use the sections that are most pertinent to your needs. However, we do encourage you to read the information that precedes the section on reacting to behaviors/interventions before reading that, as otherwise you will miss some valuable information. We want you to set the stage for success, build up a reinforcement system and try to be as proactive as possible.

Depending on your role, you might be thrown into a situation in which you are responding to a child or youth who is already engaging in serious behaviors, and you are not privy to a lot of other information. It is in these cases that you will want to review the information in Section 4 on Level 3 interventions. However, when the dust settles, so to speak, you are then encouraged to review the earlier material that pertains to the age group with which you are working.

Finally, this guide was written from two points of view—by both a professional educator and a clinical mental health provider. This is why we think it will be useful to so many people. It has information that will help kids with regard to education, of course, but also addresses the mental health issues that impact many children and teens.

BEGINNING TO SET THE STAGE FOR SUCCESS

As a part of our system development, we have established different levels of behaviors and interventions that are easy to use and follow. Level 1 behaviors are annoying and are things that we as adults really want to see change. Level 2 behaviors are starting to cause problems, are more noticeable and make adults pretty annoyed and/or nervous. Finally, Level 3 behaviors are the most serious and impact activities of daily life, learning and achievement and even may cause injury and destruction.

In our careers as teacher and therapist, we have spent much of our time with kids whose behaviors are in the Level 3 category. We are sure that this is true for many of you reading this book. There is certainly wisdom in knowing what to do when the Level 3 behaviors are taking place; however, we also acknowledge that it is important to know what to do with Level 1 and Level 2 behaviors, as they are more common. Furthermore, if we can deal with the Level 1 and 2 behaviors, we will see that Level 3 behaviors either do not happen or are mitigated due to solid programming and intervention.

Below is a display of the level system:

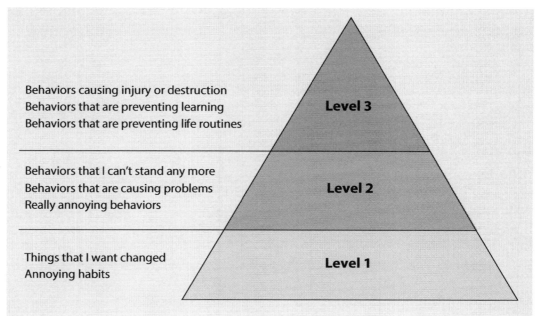

Behaviors causing injury or destruction
Behaviors that are preventing learning
Behaviors that are preventing life routines
Level 3

Behaviors that I can't stand any more
Behaviors that are causing problems
Really annoying behaviors
Level 2

Things that I want changed
Annoying habits
Level 1

Level 3 is on top of the pyramid because although the frequency is less, the intensity is greater. Level 1 is on the bottom because these behaviors involve a far greater number of kids, and the behaviors are much more frequent than Level 3 behaviors. Behaviors preventing learning and/ or success in a given environment and those causing injury or destruction are obviously the most serious and are the behaviors for which professional assistance is most frequently sought. As seen in the following diagram, behaviors escalate from Level 1 to Level 3, sometimes very quickly, unless proper programming is put in place and the correct intervention programs are used. Whether dealing with a child with severe Autism Spectrum Disorder or a youth with Oppositional Defiant Disorder, evidence-based practice is paramount in terms of providing the catalyst for safety and behavior change.

Of course, the behaviors listed in the chart on the next page are not comprehensive; however, it should be clear that behaviors exist in these levels and that it is important to match programming and interventions with behaviors. Also, we know that behaviors are processes, not static events, meaning that they can change levels very quickly and are usually continual, evolving events comprising both specific behaviors (e.g., screaming) and behaviors that interact with others (e.g., screaming and hitting self in the forehead).

Now that you see the importance of understanding the levels and what behaviors fit under each level, it becomes important to break down the behaviors in terms of what really needs to change. Honestly, sometimes behavior from a kid is more of an annoyance than anything and is really not a barrier to the child's success in that particular environment. For instance, a kid who has an annoying habit but is still doing well in the environment she is in does not really need a high level of intervention. Rather, we as the adults might need to look at why we see the behavior as annoying.

Using Levels 1, 2 and 3 provides a nice system for categorizing behaviors; however, we also want to match our program implementation with the appropriate levels. See the following chart for the types of interventions used for each level.

Level Categorization

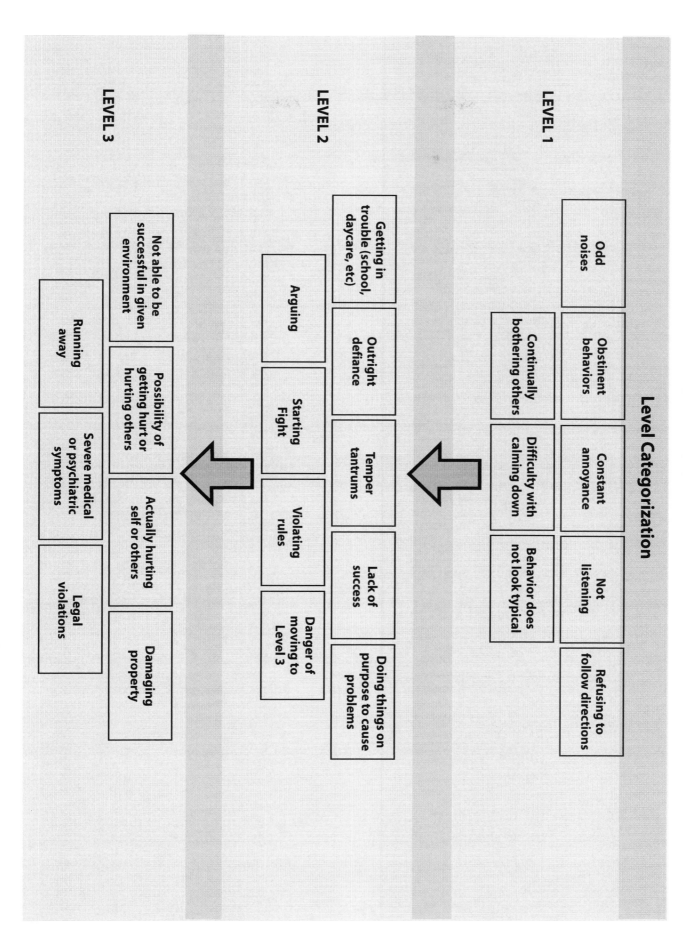

LEVEL 1

- Odd noises
- Obstinent behaviors
- Continually bothering others
- Constant annoyance
- Difficulty with calming down
- Not listening
- Behavior does not look typical
- Refusing to follow directions

LEVEL 2

- Getting in trouble (school, daycare, etc)
- Arguing
- Outright defiance
- Temper tantrums
- Starting Fight
- Violating rules
- Lack of success
- Danger of moving to Level 3
- Doing things on purpose to cause problems

LEVEL 3

- Not able to be successful in given environment
- Running away
- Possibility of getting hurt or hurting others
- Severe medical or psychiatric symptoms
- Actually hurting self or others
- Legal violations
- Damaging property

Level 1		• Planning for Success • Setting up Powerful Programs
Level 2		• Assessment • Looking at your data/assessment information • Use Motivational Schemes • Reinforcement Programs • Teaching new skills • Includes Level 1 Ideas
Level 3		• Responding to negative behaviors using reactive strategies • Higher level interventions if needed (safe room, etc.)

It is important to note that Level 2 includes the skill set(s) used in Level 1. For instance, we assume that the person in charge of programming has already set the stage for success and has considered Level 1 information before moving into the assessment/using data–information stage in Level 2. Similarly, we would expect that before someone moves into Level 3 interventions, she has considered the importance of Level 1 and Level 2 information.

◼ CHAPTER 2

Assessment: Driving Forces Behind Behaviors

To set the stage for success and help a child move toward appropriate intervention, it is important to figure out exactly where on page 5 the behavior falls. On the next page is an easy-to-use assessment that helps to break down the behaviors.

Once you know on what level the behavior falls, then you are ready to make some decisions. If a behavior falls in the Level 2 or Level 3 category, completing an assessment will be the next step in providing you with information before you begin interventions. We have included a variety of assessment tools to help you begin:

• Intake Form - Counselor/Professional (page 8)

• Intake Form - Adult/Parents (pages 10-11)

• Functional Behavior Assessment Forms including:

　　　Functional Assessment/Behavior Change Plan (pages 17-18)

　　　Individual Student Safety Plan (page 19)

　　　Intervention Plan (page 20)

　　　Parent Interview Forms (pages 22-23)

　　　Student Interview Forms (pages 24-25)

　　　Teacher Interview Form (page 26)

Behavior Management Skills Guide
Intake Form - Counselor/Professional

Name: _____   Date: _____

Describe behavior here:_____

_____

_____

Rate the behaviors marked "yes" on a 1–10 scale, with 1 being a very mild issue and 10 being a very severe issue. Behaviors marked "no" do not need to be rated.

			Rating
• Annoying habits	Yes	No	_____
• Things that I want changed	Yes	No	_____
• Really annoying behaviors	Yes	No	_____
• Behaviors that are causing problems	Yes	No	_____
• Behaviors that I can't stand any more	Yes	No	_____
• Behaviors that are preventing life routines	Yes	No	_____
• Behaviors that are preventing learning	Yes	No	_____
• Behaviors causing injury or destruction	Yes	No	_____

In terms of programming, it is important to make sure that a reinforcement system and the other success attributes are in place. This rating scale will give you a good starting point in terms of knowing at which level (Level 1, 2 or 3) to place the behaviors.

The behavior to begin with is (most severe) : _____

_____

FOR MENTAL HEALTH PROFESSIONALS

For more complicated and/or complex issues, especially involving mental health or more severe behavioral issues, more information will be needed to help guide the treatment, approach or overall protocols. In a clinical setting of any type, it is important to gather background information in an efficient manner. You should gather information about medical issues, medications, traumas, past treatment, educational issues, family issues and drug and alcohol issues. This data, often called *intake information*, is necessary to begin an appropriate course of intervention.

Many kids who engage in severe behaviors often have additional, complicating factors that make the road to success in terms of behavior management a bit bumpier. An intake form is one way to help find out needed information in order to move forth in the behavior management program. Sometimes this can be filled out by the kid if she is capable of doing so. Sometimes the parent will help, although kids seem to be more open and honest when they can at least see the form first and review it with the clinician.

You will notice that there is a symptom list as a part of the form. While not comprehensive, this list is a summary of some of the most common symptoms clinicians might see in terms of depression, anxiety and behavior issues. Depression and anxiety impact people at all ages, and if someone has severe issues in those areas, behavior management systems need to adjust accordingly.

One example of an intake form is provided (see next page). This form is typically going to be completed by the adult/parent. However, a youth capable of completing his own intake can fill it out or help fill it out.

Intake Form - Adult/Parents

Intake Information Date: _____

Name: _____ **Gender:** ____ **Age:** ____ **DOB:** _____

Parent/Guardian Name: _____

Address: _____

Reason for Intake Session: _____
_____
_____

Behavioral Concerns

☐ Noncompliance

☐ Running Away

☐ Argumentative

☐ Assaultive Behaviors

☐ Mental Health/Psychiatric Symptoms

☐ Tantrums

☐ Destruction of Property

☐ Self-Injury

☐ Other: _____

Has another mental health provider performed any services?　　Yes　　No
(Please list other providers here) _____

Has there been a previous placement at a residential, inpatient or other community setting?
Yes　　No　　If yes, please attach any summary information you may have.

Mental Health Information

- Psychiatrist: _____
- Other Agency Involvement: _____
- Past Diagnosis: _____
- Medications: _____
_____
_____

Medical Information

- Known Medical Conditions: _____
- Medications Other than Psychotropic: _____
- Other Medical Information: _____

Abuse/Neglect Information

☐ History of Physical Abuse

☐ History of Emotional Abuse

☐ History of Sexual Abuse

☐ History of Neglect

☐ History of Sexual Offending/Sexual Acting Out

☐ History of Witnessing Violence/Domestic Violence

Please Explain Any of the Above: _____

Drug/Alcohol Information

☐ Currently Using Tobacco

☐ Currently Using Alcohol

☐ Currently Using Marijuana

☐ Currently Using Other Drugs

☐ Past Usage

☐ Past Treatment/Recovery

Further Clarification: _____

Educational Information

- School/Grade: _____
- Special Education Student/Verification: _____
- History of Suspension or Expulsions: _____
- School Psychologist/Counselor/Social Worker Involvement: _____

Legal/Juvenile Justice Information

☐ Law Violations in the Community

☐ Referrals for Violations in the School Setting

☐ Diversion

☐ Probation

☐ Other: _____

Family Information

☐ Lives With One or Both Parents

☐ Lives With a Relative

☐ Lives With a Foster Parent

☐ Lives in a Group Home

☐ State Ward

☐ Caseworker Involvement: _____ Agency: _____

Symptom/Problem Checklist

Place a check mark to indicate whether a listed problem or symptom is an issue in your particular situation, then circle a ranking of its severity. Feel free to list additional problems and symptoms that are not included on this checklist.

	1=Mildly Problematic	2=Problematic	3=Very Problematic
☐ Suicidal thoughts	1	2	3
☐ Homicidal thoughts	1	2	3
☐ Past attempts at suicide	1	2	3
☐ Plans of suicide	1	2	3
☐ Thoughts of dying/death	1	2	3
☐ Anger issues	1	2	3
☐ Sadness	1	2	3
☐ Irritability	1	2	3
☐ Sleeping too much	1	2	3
☐ Sleeping too little	1	2	3
☐ Appetite problems	1	2	3
☐ Low energy	1	2	3
☐ Problems with focus	1	2	3
☐ Difficult with organization	1	2	3
☐ Panic/anxiety attacks	1	2	3
☐ Feeling nervous all the time	1	2	3
☐ Arguing/verbal fighting	1	2	3
☐ Crying/bouts of crying	1	2	3
☐ Sensitivity to light/noise/touch	1	2	3
☐ Difficulty holding still	1	2	3
☐ Feelings of shame	1	2	3
☐ Feeling worthless	1	2	3
☐ Feeling helpless	1	2	3
☐ Feeling hopeless	1	2	3
☐ Loss of sex drive/libido	1	2	3

	1=Mildly Problematic	2=Problematic	3=Very Problematic
☐ Sexual acting out	1	2	3
☐ Confusion about sexual issues	1	2	3
☐ Constantly thinking about sex	1	2	3
☐ Drinking alcohol	1	2	3
☐ Drug use	1	2	3
☐ Stealing/shoplifting	1	2	3
☐ Self-harm	1	2	3
☐ School/work difficulty	1	2	3
☐ Assaultive behaviors	1	2	3
☐ Hearing voices/seeing things	1	2	3
☐ Nightmares	1	2	3
☐ Night terrors	1	2	3

Desired Outcome

Briefly describe what you would like to happen as a result of treatment:

_____

_____

_____

_____

_____

_____

_____

Previous Strategies Attempted

Describe anything you have tried before to make the situation better:

_____

_____

_____

_____

_____

_____

_____

FUNCTIONAL BEHAVIOR ASSESSMENT

When evaluating behaviors, it is important to figure out their purpose or duty. The behavior has a job to do, a function to perform. Discovering the function of a behavior and the motivation of the individual are key to changing behavior. One tool for doing so is a Functional Behavior Assessment (FBA). We have viewed and worked with many types of FBAs. In this section, we include information that we have found to be important in the proper development of an FBA. We also include our version(s) of an FBA for your use.

When you are faced with a Level 1 behavior problem, the first thing to consider is implementation of "best practice" strategies (strategies that have been proven to be effective). Those strategies are discussed in upcoming chapters. If the behaviors of concern continue, make an educated guess about the function of the behavior. You may develop a plan related to your hypothesis or teach a new skill. However, if you aren't seeing enough change or the behavior moves to Level 2 or Level 3, you will need to take a closer look. The best way to do this is through the use of an FBA.

An FBA looks beyond the overt behavior and examines significant, child-specific, social, sensory, physical, affective, cognitive and/or environmental factors associated with the occurrence and non-occurrence of specific behaviors. This broader perspective gives you a better understanding of the purpose (function) behind the child's behavior. Interventions based on understanding why a person misbehaves are extremely useful in addressing a wide range of behavior issues.

An overview of the process of FBAs indicates the following:

- An FBA is a problem-solving tool that requires time and collaboration among professionals and parents.
- An FBA is used to look for patterns in what happens around the child just before and after the problem behavior. Examination of these patterns helps to identify the function of the behavior of concern.
- An FBA is built on the assumption that if a child keeps repeating a problem behavior, it must be serving some purpose for him, otherwise he wouldn't keep repeating it.
- The success of behavior interventions that are developed very much depends on the accurate evaluation of the behavior problem. After the function of the behavior is identified, creative problem solving is used to develop interventions that will help the child achieve the same purpose in a more appropriate or acceptable way.

So, where do you begin when conducting an FBA? The following steps are always included:

- Prioritize, describe and define the target behavior in specific, concrete terms.
- Use direct and indirect measures of behavior.
- Collect information on possible functions of the behavior of concern.
- Analyze information to form a hypothesis.
- Develop interventions/design a behavior intervention plan.
- Implement, monitor and evaluate outcomes.

After you have chosen a target behavior, it is important to define the behavior so that anyone who is observing will clearly know what the behavior of concern is for measurement purposes. The definition of the behavior needs to be precise so that we can clearly see if an intervention plan is having an impact on the behavior. Once you have defined the behavior in measurable terms, you need to take some baseline data. Baseline data determine the rate, duration or intensity of behavior before you implement strategies. You will compare these data to any changes in behavior rate, duration or intensity in order to document the success of your intervention plan.

Data should examine several factors:

- Times when the behavior does/does not occur (e.g., just prior to lunch, during a particular class in school, during transitions between classes)
- Specific location of the behavior (e.g., classroom, PE class, on the bus)
- Conditions when the behavior does/does not occur
- Setting (e.g., size of classroom, structured vs. unstructured)
- Tasks (e.g., preferred vs. nonpreferred, too challenging vs. too easy)
- Adult variables (e.g., use of effective behavioral teaching principles, not enough support)
- Individuals present when the behavior is most/least likely to occur (e.g., certain students, paraeducators)
- Events or conditions that typically occur before the behavior (e.g., assigned to a certain reading group, during discussions)
- Events or conditions that typically occur after the behavior (e.g., student is sent out of the room, student is ignored)
- Other setting events (e.g., during bad weather, during testing, sleep, allergies, sickness)
- Other behaviors that are associated with the problem behavior (e.g., series of noncompliant behaviors precedes problem behavior)
- Consider triggers that build up over time as well as more immediate triggers

Collecting Data

There are different ways to collect data that are critical in making decisions in planning interventions.

Direct Assessment. This entails actually observing the problem behavior and describing the conditions that surround the behavior (context). Often, it is necessary to have data collected across environments, people, activities, etc. Tools to help us document behavior may include the following:

- Observations: Skilled observations of the child/youth in a natural environment(s).
- Analysis of patterns of behavior: Includes frequency, duration and intensity of behaviors.
- Assessments designed to help analyze behaviors.

Indirect Assessment. This relies heavily on the use of interviews with teachers and other adults who have direct contact with the student; the interviews are semi-structured and provide critical insight into the student's perspective of the situation and lead to understanding of the reasons behind the inappropriate behavior.

Some behavior problems occur because of conflicts between the environment and the person's special needs. They may represent problems in the context in which the person must live, work and behave. An ecological analysis will help us understand the match between the environment and the child/student that could be impacting the behavior of concern.

After collecting data, we should be able to start answering some questions regarding the behavior of concern, such as the following:

- What purpose does the behavior serve?
- What personal and environmental risk factors (difficulties) are related to this behavior?
- What is the pattern of the behavior's occurrence?

The next step in the FBA is forming a hypothesis as why the behavior is occurring. This will lead us in choosing strategies to decrease the behaviors of concern and give the child/student more appropriate ways to interact in her environment. We can begin to look at several ways of categorizing why a behavior is occurring, based on our direct and indirect assessment information. Possible functions of behavior or reasons why behavior is occurring include the following:

- To obtain/gain something desired
- To avoid something/escape from something
- To communicate something

Behavior can also indicate the following:

- **Skill deficit:** A behavioral or academic skill the student does not know how to perform. Example: In a disagreement, the student hits another student because he does not know other strategies for conflict resolution.
- **Performance deficit:** A behavioral or academic skill the student does know but does not consistently perform. Example: A student is chronically late for the classes she doesn't "like." In general, "can't" indicates a skill deficit, whereas "won't" indicates a performance deficit.
- **Pain:** Emotional or physical pain.
- **Sensory deficits:** Acting out to get sensory needs met.
- **Control issues:** Acting out to maintain control. This is part of the "gains something" category.

Functional Behavior Assessment
Change Plan

Name: _____

Date of Birth: _____ Gender/Age: _____

Description/Definition of Problem Behavior Based on Direct Observation or Report From Primary Caregiver:

Child/Youth Behavior: _____
_____

Parent/Provider Behavior: _____
_____

Starting Information

How often does the behavior occur?: _____
_____

How long does the behavior last? _____
_____

On a scale of 1–10, how intense is the behavior? _____

What makes the behavior worse/aggravates the behavior? _____

Triggers to Behavior Described Above? _____
_____

What Are the Results of Behavior? _____

What happens to the child/youth as a result of the behavior? _____
_____

What happens to the parent/provider as a result of the behavior? _____
_____

Duty of the Behavior (What does child/youth gain/avoid/communicate to others?)

    Function for Child/Youth: _____

    Does the Behavior Serve Any Function for an Adult Involved? _____
    _____

    New Behaviors (Appropriate alternative behaviors to achieve same function): _____
    _____

Behavior Change Plan

    Objective of the New Plan: _____
    _____
    _____
    _____

    How Is the New Behavior Going to Be Taught? _____
    _____
    _____
    _____

    What Skill(s) Does the Parent/Provider Need? _____
    _____
    _____
    _____

    How Is the New Behavior Going to Be Reinforced? Is Everyone on Board? _____
    _____
    _____
    _____

    Is an Alternative Discipline Plan Needed? (This means that the usual way of discipline is not working or is inappropriate.) Yes/No (If yes, use Safety Plan, Next Page) _____

Individual Student Safety Plan

> An individual student safety plan, unlike a typical behavior plan, addresses specific behavior that is dangerous to the student or others

Name: _____

Date Plan Was Initiated: _____ Review Dates: _____

Medical/Psychiatric/Mental Health Information:

Medical Alert: _____

Other Information: _____

Description of Specific Unsafe Behaviors:

Warning Signs/Triggers	Strategies That Work	Strategies That Don't Work

Crisis Response Plan

What to do if the student exhibits above described behavior:	Who will do what/back up staff?

Student Safety Team Members: (Include IEP Team, Paraeducators, Administrator, Nurse, Parent/Guardian)

Name/Signature	Title	Date
_____	_____	_____
_____	_____	_____
_____	_____	_____
_____	_____	_____

Functional Behavior Assessment
Intervention Plan - School

Name: _____ Date of Birth: _____ Grade:_____

Address:_____ Gender: _____ Age: _____

School: _____ Date of Notice:_____

Description/Definition Of Problem Behavior Based On Direct Observation _____
_____
_____

Baseline Information (Frequency, Duration, Intensity, Latency, etc.): _____
_____
_____

Setting Events (What makes the behavior worse): _____
_____
_____

Antecedents To Behavior Described Above: _____
_____
_____

Current Consequence(S)/Responses For The Behavior(S): _____
_____
_____

Function Of The Problem Behavior: (What Does Student Gain/Avoid/Communicate?) _____
_____
_____

Replacement Behaviors: (Appropriate Alternative Behaviors To Achieve Same Function) _____
_____
_____

Behavioral Goals Incorporating Replacement Behaviors: _____
_____
_____

Skill Building: (Examples: Problem-Solving, Conflict Resolution, Decision-Making, Negotiation/Mediation, Social Skills Training, Relaxation/Impulse/Anger Control Skills) _____
_____
_____

Specific Teaching Strategies And Supports (Including Staff Support): _____
_____
_____

Modifications: (Examples: Program, Curricular, Instructional Materials, Seating, Removing Seductive Items, Restricting Access To Environments, Alternative Site For Instruction To Reduce Stressors/Stimulation) _____
_____
_____
_____

Components Of Student's Positive Reinforcement Plan: _____
_____
_____

Data Collection Plan: (List/Describe System To Monitor Replacement Behavior And To Document Progress Toward Desired Criteria) _____
_____
_____

Crisis Intervention Plan: (If Yes, Describe In Safety Plan) _____
_____
_____

Task   Person Responsible

Informing All Parties Of Their Responsbilities In Implementing Plan _____

Monitoring Progress Through Date Collection _____

Scheduling Reviews To Discuss Progress _____

Modifying Or Providing Modified Materials _____

Other: _____

Evaluation Date(s):_____
_____
_____
_____

Functional Behavior Assessment
Parent Interview Form

Name: _____ Date: _____

Parent/Guardian: _____ Date: _____

Target Behavior: _____

Child's Strengths	Child's Interests	Child Learns Best With Tasks That Involve
☐ Friendly ☐ Honest ☐ A good helper ☐ Good sense of humor ☐ Kind to adults ☐ Kind to children/peers ☐ A leader ☐ Other:_____ ☐ Other:_____ ☐ Other:_____		☐ Computer ☐ Writing ☐ Oral responses ☐ Working with others ☐ Working alone ☐ Artistic expression ☐ Hands-on projects ☐ Other: _____ ☐ Other: _____ ☐ Other: _____
Behavior Occurs When:	What Is Your Reaction to the Behavior?	What Things Are Reinforcers for Your Child?
☐ Asked to follow a direction ☐ It's time for homework ☐ Asked to do a chore or helping task ☐ There's a time limit (e.g., curfew, being on time) ☐ Told "no" or "stop" ☐ Corrected ☐ Around a certain peer group ☐ There is a transition ☐ Things are unstructured ☐ Other:_____ ☐ Other:_____ ☐ Other:_____		

Functional Behavior Assessment
Parent Interview Form

Name: _____ Grade: _____ Date: _____

Informant: _____

1. Behavior of concern:

_____

_____

2. When did you first notice the behavior occurring?

_____

_____

3. Were there any changes at home or in the student's life when this behavior began?

_____

_____

4. When does the behavior occur?

_____

_____

5. When does the behavior <u>not</u> occur?

_____

_____

6. What do you usually do when the behavior occurs?

_____

_____

7. Does that help?

_____

_____

8. Have you noticed things that make the behavior worse?

_____

_____

9. Is there any other information you want to share about the behavior of concern?

_____

_____

Functional Behavior Assessment
Student Interview Form

Name: _____ Grade: _____ Date: _____

Behavior: _____

When do you think you have the <u>fewest</u> problems with the behavior listed?

_____

_____

When do you think you have the <u>most</u> problems with the behavior listed?

_____

_____

What happens when you do the behavior listed?

_____

_____

Who is around you when you display the listed behavior?

_____

_____

What are your favorite activities/subjects at school?

_____

_____

What are your hobbies or interests?

_____

_____

If you could change one thing at school to help you out, what would it be?

_____

_____

Anything else you want us to know that affects your behavior?

_____

_____

Functional Behavior Assessment
Student Interview Form

Name: _____ Grade: _____ Date: _____

Behavior: _____

School:			**I learn best with tasks that involve:**
1. Is too hard	☐ Yes	☐ No	☐ Computer
			☐ Writing
2. Is too easy/boring	☐ Yes	☐ No	☐ Oral responses
			☐ Working with others
3. Has too much homework	☐ Yes	☐ No	☐ Working alone
			☐ Artistic expression
4. Has rewards for good work	☐ Yes	☐ No	☐ Hands-on projects
			☐ Other: _____
5. Teachers are interested in me	☐ Yes	☐ No	☐ Other: _____
			☐ Other: _____

I do the listed behavior when:

I don't do the behavior when:

My reinforcers or rewards are:

Functional Behavior Assessment
Teacher Interview Form

Name: _____ Grade: _____ Date: _____

Teacher: _____ Date: _____

Target Behavior: _____

Student strengths:	Student interests:	Student learns best with tasks that involve:
☐ Friendly		☐ Computer
☐ Honest		☐ Writing
☐ A good helper		☐ Oral responses
☐ Good sense of humor		☐ Working with others
☐ Kind to adults		☐ Working alone
☐ Kind to children/peers		☐ Artistic expression
☐ A leader		☐ Hands-on projects
☐ Other:_____		☐ Limited paper/pencil tasks
☐ Other:_____		☐ Job skills/service learning projects
☐ Other:_____		☐ Other:_____
		☐ Other:_____
		☐ Other:_____

Behavior occurs when:	What is your reaction to the behavior?	What things are reinforcers for your student?
☐ Asked to follow a direction		
☐ Tasks are difficult		
☐ Not prepared with materials		
☐ There's a time limit		
☐ There's a change in routine		
☐ Told "no" or "stop"		
☐ Corrected		
☐ Around a certain peer group		
☐ There is a transition		
☐ Things are unstructured		
☐ Other: _____		
☐ Other: _____		
☐ Other: _____		

■ CHAPTER 3

Motivational Schemes and Reinforcement Systems

INTRODUCTION TO MOTIVATIONAL SCHEMES

In order to set up behavior programs and reinforcement plans that are appropriate and effective, professionals need to understand the motivations that people have for maintaining, changing or eliminating their behaviors. Motivational schemes have been established to help describe and detail the different ways we all are motivated. Usually, we are motivated by a combination of factors—rarely is a behavior related 100% to one motivational scheme. Remember that by the time you are creating behavior programs, you will have an understanding as to why a behavior occurs, which you will have gained through completing a FBA. The following sections describe how to change behavior based on understanding a person's motivation.

Internal (Intrinsic) and External (Extrinsic)

In general, internal motivation comes from the feelings people have as a result of a behavior. These feelings range from a sense of mastery and satisfaction to a sense of control and contentment. So, a person who feels a sense of satisfaction, mastery or control from a certain behavior is essentially internally motivated by that behavior.

By contrast, external motivation comes from things or privileges that a person may receive. For instance, getting a paycheck is an external motivation, as is earning a sticker, a star or a privilege to do something. Standard token economies are wonderful for students who are externally motivated; many behavior plans rely on external motivation systems.

As stated earlier, usually people have a combination of motivational factors. The trick is to find out what a person's dominant motivational scheme is in order to set up the right reinforcement and/or behavior management plan.

Examples of internal motivation:
- A sense of mastery/realization of an accomplishment
- Programs that create a sense of satisfaction
- Self-achievement, resulting in confidence
- Received praise or acknowledgement
- Helping others, then feeling good about doing so

Examples of external motivation:
- Token economies
- Stickers, good marks, etc.
- Behavioral charts
- Trophies, stripes, badges, etc.
- Money or other material items

Social and Emotional

Based on our personalities, environment and situations, we all have varying degrees of social and emotional needs and motivating factors. Some people are motivated by being included in large group activities and social events, whereas others are motivated by having moments of solitude and quiet time. Also, everyone has different emotional needs, and getting these needs met is a major factor in behavior continuance, modification or elimination.

Examples of social and emotional schemes:

- Belonging to a peer group
- Being cared for/feeling loved and appreciated
- Belonging to a community, group, society, etc.
- Feeling safe and attached to others/bonding with caregivers
- Having friends, pleasant social contacts

Attention

The motivation to receive attention from others is another primary motivational scheme. With younger children, the motivation is usually to earn attention from the parent(s). Later, receiving attention from other adults becomes important. Still later, attention from a peer group is sought. As a person matures, receiving attention from a larger group/community and for personal/ professional accomplishments also can be become important. At a basic level, any attention is better than no attention, and neglect or absence of any attention (even if negative) is devastating.

Examples of attention schemes:

- Being recognized as an important person
- Being noticed for behavior (preferably positive behavior)
- Receiving acknowledgements for accomplishments, milestones and life events
- Recognition of positive behavioral and personality attributes

Control

All people are motivated to some extent by the need to have control. The need to have control over oneself is very powerful. With children who have trauma histories, attachment issues and other challenges, the need for control is ever more powerful, even to the point of desperation. When actual control is not appropriate or allowed, the perceived sense of control ("I can choose this or that") can be just as important. Often, our perception is as powerful as reality. In terms of behavioral programs, allowing for a sense of control and choice will result in better behavior overall and a much better chance at actual sustained behavioral change.

Examples of control schemes:

- Control over one's environment and/or schedule
- Power over decisions/the ability to make choices
- Control over emotions, reactions and life situations

Sensory

Regardless of whether someone is aware of his sensory issues, it is very important that sensory issues are addressed in terms of motivation. In other words, the sensory needs can be a strong motivational factor in determining behavior. The basic sensory need of being warmer or cooler can be a motivation for behavior. Obviously, sensory needs are a vast and complex area, so simplifying the discussion of them is not easy. We all have varying degrees of sensory needs, and in general, individuals on the autism spectrum have even greater sensitivity to sensory stimuli. The importance of meeting at least basic sensory needs cannot be underestimated.

Examples of sensory schemes:

- Getting physical needs met
- Having hearing levels increased or reduced
- Visual adjustments
- Avoiding or acquiring pleasant smells
- Eating desired foods/avoiding undesired foods

Pain

Basically, we all want to avoid pain whether the pain is emotional or physical. If we are in pain (especially physical), our behavior will completely be altered by the level of discomfort we feel. Therefore, a plan that helps someone lesson or eliminate pain will be highly motivating to her in terms of helping with her behavior. Even the chance to avoid future pain can be highly motivating. This is one reason why substances can be so attractive: They help people avoid current pain as well as future pain.

Examples of pain schemes:

- Avoiding pain altogether
- Getting assistance when in physical pain (e.g., medication, adjustments)
- Appropriate care for emotional pain

Fear (Avoiding Fears)

In general, if we can avoid the things we are afraid of, we are motivated by the behavior that allows that. Thus, if someone has strong anxiety when engaging (or even thinking about engaging in) a certain behavior, he will be motivated by something or someone that helps him avoid or lessen that fear. For instance, if a student has a fear of speaking in front of others and we help him through that process, we are providing some motivation for him. Or, if a young child will not go to bed because of a fear of the dark, then a nightlight becomes very reinforcing for her.

Examples of fear schemes:

- Allowing someone to avoid the fear entirely
- Mitigating the actual fear
- Developing coping skills for fears
- Accommodating for real or imagined fears

Escape

When a person escapes from his environment, for example leaving the classroom, the reason for this behavior can have several causes:

1. To leave the environment because what he is doing is too hard or he perceives that he cannot do the work. Perceived incompetence is the same in a young person's mind as actual incompetence.
2. Escape because he is confused.
3. Escape to get attention (also feeds into attention schemes)
4. Escape to gain control (also feeds into control schemes)
5. Simply dislikes the environment he is in

Examples of escape schemes:

- Escape-based plans (times when escapes are assigned)
- Special jobs, passes and other appropriate escapes
- Creating different environments
- Making current situation more reinforcing

REINFORCEMENT PLANS

Reinforcement plans that are effective need to match the motivation of the individual as much as possible. Sometimes, plans are put in place and are labeled ineffective or, worse, the student or client is identified as resistant or noncompliant. Actually, what is more likely the case is that the reinforcement plan does not fit the motivational scheme for that person. An easy example to understand is the following: Student A is motivated in general by having control and feeling satisfied by doing creative work/independent work. She is placed on a reinforcement plan that is based on a standard system of earning plusses for following directions and completing tasks. This student does not progress or advance. The reason is that for the most part, she is not motivated by earning the plusses but would be motivated by being given a better sense of control (even if perceived) and also by being recognized for her creative spark.

Fitting Motivational Schemes with Reinforcement Plans

As stated earlier, to develop the correct reinforcement plan, it is important to figure out how a person is motivated. In some cases, it is easy to determine someones motivation. In such cases, the reinforcement plan becomes easier to develop. We have developed a motivational assessment tool for your use in situations in which it is more difficult to discover motivation. The Assessment of Motivational Schemes (AMS) tool is an easy-to-use brief assessment designed to help you quickly narrow down some motivational patterns/schemes to later use in a reinforcement plan.

For those of you working with older children and teens who are able to understand vocabulary (written or verbal), the AMS self-assessment, AMS(SA), might be another useful tool. We recommend you use the AMS tool first and then decide if you want to use the AMS(SA) version as well. Following are copies of the AMS and AMS(SA).

Assessment of Motivation
Counselor/Professional Questionnaire

Name: _____ Grade: _____ Date: _____

Person Completing Assessment: _____

Behavior Description: _____

Instructions: This is a questionnaire designed to identify motivational factors/schemes behind child/youth behaviors. Essentially, what does the child/youth need or want through their behavior and what motivates them to change? From this information, more specific programs and systems can be developed for reinforcement and behavior change. Read each statement/question and then circle the answer that fits best. Then, the scores can be totaled for an estimate of which motivational scheme(s) are most pertinent.

Child or youth is motivated by:	0= Never	1= Seldom	2= Sometimes	3= Half the time	4= Often	5= Almost Aways
Intrinsic vs. Extrinsic						
1. A sense of mastery?	0	1	2	3	4	5
2. Realization of an accomplishment?	0	1	2	3	4	5
3. A sense of satisfaction?	0	1	2	3	4	5
4. Self-achievement, thus confidence?	0	1	2	3	4	5
5. Receiving praise or acknowledgement?	0	1	2	3	4	5
6. Helping others and feeling good about it?	0	1	2	3	4	5
7. Token economies?	0	1	2	3	4	5
8. Stickers, good marks, etc.?	0	1	2	3	4	5
9. Behavioral charts?	0	1	2	3	4	5
10. Trophies, stripes, badges, etc.?	0	1	2	3	4	5
11. Money or other material items?	0	1	2	3	4	5
Social/Emotional						
12. Belonging to a peer group?	0	1	2	3	4	5
13. Being cared for/feeling loved and appreciated?	0	1	2	3	4	5
14. Belonging to a community, group, society, etc.?	0	1	2	3	4	5
15. Feeling safe, attached/bonded with caregivers?	0	1	2	3	4	5
16. Having friends, pleasant social contacts?	0	1	2	3	4	5
Attention						
17. Being recognized as an important person?	0	1	2	3	4	5
18. Being noticed for behavior?	0	1	2	3	4	5
19. Receiving acknowledgements (praise, etc.)?	0	1	2	3	4	5
20. Recognition of personal attributes?	0	1	2	3	4	5

	0= Never	1= Seldom	2= Sometimes	3= Half the time	4= Often	5= Almost Aways
Control						
21. Control over one's environment?	0	1	2	3	4	5
22. Control over routine and/or schedule?	0	1	2	3	4	5
23. Power over decisions?	0	1	2	3	4	5
24. The ability to make choices?	0	1	2	3	4	5
25. Control over emotions?	0	1	2	3	4	5
26. Controls reactions to emotional situations?	0	1	2	3	4	5
Sensory						
27. Getting physical needs met?	0	1	2	3	4	5
28. Having hearing levels increased or reduced?	0	1	2	3	4	5
29. Visual adjustments?	0	1	2	3	4	5
30. Avoiding bad/acquiring pleasant smells?	0	1	2	3	4	5
31. Eating desired foods/avoiding undesired foods?	0	1	2	3	4	5
Pain						
32. Avoiding pain altogether?	0	1	2	3	4	5
33. Getting assistance when in physical pain?	0	1	2	3	4	5
34. Assistance with medication, adjustments, etc.?	0	1	2	3	4	5
35. Appropriate care for emotional pain?	0	1	2	3	4	5
Fear						
36. Avoiding the fear entirely?	0	1	2	3	4	5
37. Mitigating the actual fear?	0	1	2	3	4	5
38. Developing coping skills for fears?	0	1	2	3	4	5
39. Accommodating for real or imagined fears?	0	1	2	3	4	5
Escape						
40. Leaving environments provides satisfaction	0	1	2	3	4	5
41. Escaping due to perceived incompetence	0	1	2	3	4	5
42. Leaving environment due to confusion	0	1	2	3	4	5
43. Leaving to gain control or attention	0	1	2	3	4	5

Totals: Add up totals for each section.

1–6:	Score: _____	Score of 19–30 is significant
7–11:	Score: _____	Score of 13–20 is significant
12–16:	Score: _____	Score of 16–25 is significant
17–20:	Score: _____	Score of 12–20 is significant
21–26:	Score: _____	Score of 19–30 is significant
27–31:	Score: _____	Score of 16–25 is significant
32–35:	Score: _____	Score of 13–20 is significant
36–39:	Score: _____	Score of 13–20 is significant
40–43:	Score: _____	Score of 13–20 is significant

Scores within 3 points of the maximum score are prominent. Areas with high scores indicate likelihood that the particular area is a strong motivational scheme. If a number of areas have high scores, behavior planning needs to take a comprehensive approach.

Comments: _____

_____

_____

Assessment of Motivation
Student/Self-Assessment Questionnaire

Student: _____ Grade: _____ Date: _____

Person Completing Assessment: _____

Instructions: This is a questionnaire designed to identify motivational factors/schemes behind child/youth behaviors. Essentially, what does the child/youth need or want through their behavior and what motivates them to change? From this information, more specific programs and systems can be developed for reinforcement and behavior change. Read each statement/question and then circle the answer that fits best. Then, the scores can be totaled for an estimate of which motivational scheme(s) are most pertinent. **This assessment is for the youth to answer directly, either by filling it out or by answering the items read by another person. It should only be used when the youth can engage in dialogue in order to fully understand each item.**

Are you motivated/excited or feel better by:	0= Never	1= Seldom	2= Sometimes	3= Half the time	4= Often	5= Almost Aways
Intrinsic vs. Extrinsic						
1. Mastering something?	0	1	2	3	4	5
2. Realizing an accomplishment?	0	1	2	3	4	5
3. Feeling satisfied about doing things?	0	1	2	3	4	5
4. Self-achievement, thus confidence?	0	1	2	3	4	5
5. Receiving praise or acknowledgement?	0	1	2	3	4	5
6. Helping others and feeling good about it?	0	1	2	3	4	5
7. Earning chips, coins, tokens, etc.?	0	1	2	3	4	5
8. Earning stickers, good marks, etc.?	0	1	2	3	4	5
9. Having a goal sheet or behavioral charts?	0	1	2	3	4	5
10. Trophies, stripes, badges, etc.?	0	1	2	3	4	5
11. Money or other material items?	0	1	2	3	4	5
Social/Emotional						
12. Belonging to a peer group?	0	1	2	3	4	5
13. Being cared for/feeling loved and appreciated?	0	1	2	3	4	5
14. Belonging to a community, group, society, etc.?	0	1	2	3	4	5
15. Feeling safe, attached/bonded with caregivers?	0	1	2	3	4	5
16. Having friends, pleasant social contacts?	0	1	2	3	4	5
Attention						
17. Being recognized as an important person?	0	1	2	3	4	5
18. Being noticed for behavior?	0	1	2	3	4	5
19. Receiving acknowledgements (praise, etc.)?	0	1	2	3	4	5
20. Being recognized for personal attributes?	0	1	2	3	4	5
Control						
21. Control over your environment?	0	1	2	3	4	5
22. Control over routine and/or schedule?	0	1	2	3	4	5
23. Have power over decisions?	0	1	2	3	4	5
24. The ability to make choices?	0	1	2	3	4	5
25. Control over emotions?	0	1	2	3	4	5
26. Controls reactions to emotional situations?	0	1	2	3	4	5

	0= Never	1= Seldom	2= Sometimes	3= Half the time	4= Often	5= Almost Aways
Sensory						
27. Getting your physical needs met?	0	1	2	3	4	5
28. Having hearing levels increased or reduced?	0	1	2	3	4	5
29. Having visual adjustments?	0	1	2	3	4	5
30. Avoiding bad/acquiring pleasant smells?	0	1	2	3	4	5
31. Eating desired foods/avoiding undesired foods?	0	1	2	3	4	5
Pain						
32. Avoiding pain altogether?	0	1	2	3	4	5
33. Getting assistance when in physical pain?	0	1	2	3	4	5
34. Getting help with medication, adjustments, etc.?	0	1	2	3	4	5
35. Getting help for emotional pain?	0	1	2	3	4	5
Fear						
36. Avoiding the fear entirely?	0	1	2	3	4	5
37. Making the actual fear less?	0	1	2	3	4	5
38. Developing coping skills for fears?	0	1	2	3	4	5
39. Adjusting for real or imagined fears?	0	1	2	3	4	5
Escape						
40. Leaving environments provides satisfaction	0	1	2	3	4	5
41. Escaping due to perceived incompetence	0	1	2	3	4	5
42. Leaving environment due to confusion	0	1	2	3	4	5
43. Leaving to gain control or attention	0	1	2	3	4	5

Totals: Add up totals for each section.

1–6:	Score: _____	Score of 19–30 is significant
7–11:	Score: _____	Score of 13–20 is significant
12–16:	Score: _____	Score of 16–25 is significant
17–20:	Score: _____	Score of 12–20 is significant
21–26:	Score: _____	Score of 19–30 is significant
27–31:	Score: _____	Score of 16–25 is significant
32–35:	Score: _____	Score of 13–20 is significant
36–39:	Score: _____	Score of 13–20 is significant
40–43:	Score: _____	Score of 13–20 is significant

Scores within 3 points of the maximum score are prominent. Areas with high scores indicate likelihood that the particular area is a strong motivational scheme. If a number of areas have high scores, behavior planning needs to take a comprehensive approach.

Comments: _____

_____

_____

Reinforcement

Once a motivational pattern is discovered, it is much easier to begin to develop a formal or informal behavior program. Of course, there are multiple avenues by which behavior is reinforced, but it is critical to look at the most dominant or most important motivational pattern discovered during assessment.

Whether you are reinforcing behavior in a whole group of kids or have an individualized reinforcement plan set up with one child, the concepts are similar. A reinforcer is any item or event that increases the rate of a behavior when it is presented following the behavior. So, if you praise your child and give her an allowance for helping with dinner dishes, you are reinforcing that behavior, and your child will probably continue to engage in that cleaning behavior in the future. We need to reinforce desired behavior frequently. Typically, we want to aim for implementing five to six times as many interactions following desired behavior as following undesired behavior.

Reinforcement usually makes people think of various types of rewards; however, it is important to remember that rewards are not always reinforcing. Sometimes a great reward can follow a behavior, but the behavior does not increase. In such cases, the reward is not a reinforcer—it is only a reinforcer if the behavior it follows increases. Avoid assuming that something is a reinforcer simply because it is something most people like. It may not be reinforcing for that particular learner of the specific behavior being taught.

Positive reinforcers may involve some form of sensory experience, social interaction, activity or access to a tangible item. Sensory-based reinforcers follow a behavior and provide pleasurable sensations of sound, taste, small, sight, movement or touch. Sensory-based reinforcement can include preferred music, water play, a flashlight, colorful liquid timers, objects that glitter, bubbles, lotions, rocking in a chair, vibrating objects or a quiet time or place. Occupational therapists are a great resource to consult when considering using sensory items for reinforcement.

Adults need to recognize that some individuals exhibit misbehavior to engage your attention. Manage social interactions by providing positive attention for desired behaviors and avoiding social interaction in response to inappropriate behaviors. Adults need to recognize what behaviors are safe to ignore and which ones are not. In addition to giving attention for positive behaviors, setting up times when a child can spend some time with a preferred person or be a helper with other students or adults are easy ways to use social interactions as reinforcement.

An *activity reinforcer* is simply being able to participate in a preferred activity. This may be a video game, a puzzle, a computer game, play time with a pet, a favorite toy or earning a preferred job responsibility. Activity reinforcers are usually given following multiple occurrences of appropriate behavior or task completion.

Tangible reinforcers are objects, which are given to an individual following a desired behavior. Tangibles are often edible items. Often, adults use tangible reinforcement for persons who are developmentally challenged, but let's face it—we all enjoy a treat sometimes! Tangible reinforcers are the most artificial form of positive reinforcement; however, occasional use of tangible reinforcers with any individual can be effective when teaching a new behavior or when working with a behavior that is very difficult for the person to perform. Adults want to avoid relying solely on tangible reinforcers for most individuals. Expanding the reinforcement repertoire for any person is most desirable so that he has multiple options of reinforcement at various times during the day.

Token systems of reinforcement are common with both groups of kids and individual children. Token reinforcement is a system in which an object or visual symbol is provided following a desired behavior. This object or symbol is not inherently reinforcing but is used to trade for a different item that is reinforcing. Point systems and level systems are highly abstract and more complex versions of token systems. Token systems delay the receipt of the reinforcer. Individuals who participate in token systems need to be able to understand visual symbols and be able to delay gratification. You will see many examples of token systems in the upcoming chapters.

No matter what form of reinforcement you are utilizing, there are some important points to remember:

- Reinforcers should be delivered immediately and be small and varied over time.

- Provide higher-level reinforcers for best-quality responding or for a difficult response. The response effort will affect the level of motivation. The reinforcer must be worth it to the person for a more difficult response, especially if other reinforcers are available for less work.

- Use specific praise, especially for learners with language issues. Many times, kids don't readily understand why you are telling them "Good job!" or "Way to go!" Make sure to attach the reason why to help the child understand what exactly is being reinforced; e.g., "Nice job doing your math problems!" or "I like the way you are waiting your turn." (Language changes when working with children with attachment disorder.)

- Use a variety of reinforcers and small amounts to avoid satiation. Motivation can change from moment to moment, and reinforcers lose their value if they are used over and over again.

- Generally, new behaviors will be learned more rapidly if they are reinforced every time they occur. In terms of a new response, behavior that produces an immediate consequence will be more strongly affected by the reinforcer than when the consequence is delayed.

- Anticipation of participating in desired activities will be most effective when represented visually. For reinforcement that will be delayed, visual representation will need to be present. This can be on a visual schedule that shows what tasks earn reinforcers, how many behaviors need to occur, etc. before the reinforcement will occur. Token reinforcement systems are a perfect example of how visuals can be used to show when a reinforcer will be earned.

- When using activity-based reinforcers that do not have a discrete beginning or end, use a kitchen timer, digital timer or sand timer to indicate when the activity is finished. If the activity is shooting hoops, for example, it needs to be timed to indicate its beginning and end.

We suggest teaching the concept of "my turn" when working with some children who have a hard time giving up a reinforcing item or quitting a reinforcing activity. When a child has a reinforcer in hand, say "my turn" as you remove the item just for a moment before returning it to the child. Keep working on this concept as you keep the item for a little bit longer each time. Eventually, the child will know that when you say "my turn," and take the reinforcer that she will be getting it back soon.

An easy way to identify reinforcers for kids is to do a reinforcer assessment. This can be accomplished in several ways. Having the student or a parent complete or respond to questions on reinforcement inventories is an easy way to discern what is reinforcing for a student. We have included several examples of reinforcement inventories in this section. Other ways of assessment include having a variety of items available on a table and seeing what the student engages with first, second, etc. Let the student have the chosen item for a short time and then move on to see what else is reinforcing to that individual. Also, it's very easy to simply watch what kids seem to gravitate toward and play with during free time as a way to identify potential reinforcers.

Typically, there are two ways that reinforcement is delivered. Continuous reinforcement is delivered following every occurrence of the targeted behavior. Intermittent reinforcement is when some but not all of the occurrences of the targeted response are reinforced. Intermittent reinforcement is the most common type, but if you are trying to establish a reinforcement plan for a child with a Level 2 or 3 set of behaviors, you will probably be starting off with a continuous schedule of reinforcement and then moving to an intermittent schedule of reinforcement.

A final reminder about reinforcement: As stated previously, understanding the motivation an individual has is highly integrated with developing an appropriate reinforcement plan. Sometimes, motivation and reinforcers are easily matched. Other times, the motivation and reinforcers are less tangible. This is more common with older children and teenagers.

Examples of Reinforcement Inventories

Following are several different examples of methods to find out specific reinforcers for different types of situations. Ideally, we want the reinforcement to fit the motivation of the individual.

Inventories - Elementary

Things your child likes to eat

_____

_____

_____

_____

Things your child likes to drink

_____

_____

_____

Activities your child likes (watching TV, spinning, sitting in a special chair, squeezing)

_____

_____

_____

_____

Toys your child likes

_____

_____

_____

_____

Social games your child likes (peek-a-boo, chase, tickling)

_____

_____

_____

Places your child likes to visit (store, zoo, grandparents' home)

_____

_____

_____

_____

What your child chooses to do during "free time"

_____

_____

_____

Reinforcer Assessment
Inventories - Secondary

Things your child likes to eat

_____
_____
_____
_____

Things your child likes to drink

_____
_____
_____

Subject your child likes

_____
_____
_____

Computer/video games your child likes

_____
_____
_____

After-school activities your child likes

_____
_____
_____

Places your child likes to hang out

_____
_____
_____

What your child chooses to do during "free time"

_____
_____
_____

Reinforcer Assessment
Inventories - Tangibles

Name: _____ Date: _____

Instructions: Use a check mark (✓) to indicate the items preferred.

TANGIBLE ITEMS	List preferred types:
☐ Chips	
☐ Cookies	
☐ Candy	
☐ Fruit	
☐ Cereal	
☐ Other snacks	
☐ Drinks	
☐ Other preferred foods	
☐ Stickers	
☐ Toys	
☐ Games	
☐ Other preferred items	

Inventories - Social/Sensory

Name: _____ Date: _____

Instructions: Use a check mark (✓) to indicate the items preferred.

Social And Sensory Reinforcers

☐ Adult attention

☐ Attention from specific adults

   List preferred adults: _____

☐ Being left alone

☐ Time spent with peer

   List preferred peers: _____

☐ Freedom from interference from adults

☐ Freedom from interference from peers

☐ A positive note to give to a person of choice

☐ Hugs	☐ Praise	☐ Eye contact
☐ Private praise	☐ Public recognition	☐ Public praise
☐ Being rocked	☐ Being held	☐ Applause
☐ OK sign	☐ Back rub	☐ Tickles
☐ Sit in adult's lap	☐ Thumbs up sign	☐ Shake hands
☐ High five sign	☐ Pats	☐ Twirling around
☐ Swinging	☐ Being brushed	☐ Jumping
☐ Vibrating item	☐ Lotion	☐ Powder
☐ Roll up in blanket	☐ Smiles	☐ Motor lab
☐ Blowing bubbles	☐ Shoes off	☐ Cologne
☐ Stress balls	☐ Light-up toys	☐ Spinning toys
☐ Shiny objects	☐ Snow globes	☐ Wind-up toys
☐ Party blowers	☐ Books with sound effects	☐ Fans
☐ Bubble wrap	☐ Feathers	☐ Play Dough®/Silly Putty®
☐ Sand play	☐ Water play	☐ Tearing paper
☐ Ball pit	☐ Bumble ball	

☐ Other: _____

☐ Other: _____

☐ Other: _____

☐ Other: _____

☐ Other: _____

Reinforcer Assessment
Inventories - Activity

Name: _____ Date: _____

Instructions: Use a check mark (✓) to indicate the items preferred.

Activity Reinforcers

☐ Music

   List preferred music: _____

☐ Playing with toys

   List preferred toys: _____

☐ Puzzles	☐ Computer	☐ Water play
☐ Outside play	☐ Snack time	☐ Free time
☐ Playing with pets	☐ Riding toys	☐ Books, stories
☐ Going for a walk	☐ Making choices	☐ Helping adult
☐ Car/marble ramps	☐ Painting	☐ Being read to
☐ Job responsibilities	☐ Wearing cosmetics	☐ Drawing
☐ Wearing jewelry	☐ Special seat	☐ Balloons
☐ More independence	☐ Riding bikes	☐ Cooking
☐ Stamp/stamp pad	☐ Trains	☐ Beads
☐ Magnadoodle®	☐ Viewfinder	☐ Dress up
☐ Trampoline	☐ Rocking chair	☐ Dancing
☐ Swinging	☐ Therapy balls	☐ Scooter
☐ Skates, Rollerblades	☐ Bowling	☐ Air hockey
☐ Sit and Spin	☐ Wagon rides	☐ Cards

☐ List preferred materials: _____

☐ Computer

   List preferred programs: _____

☐ Social activities

   List preferred types: _____

☐ Video games

   List preferred games: _____

☐ Leisure activities

   List preferred types: _____

Reinforcer Assessment
Inventories - Interest Area

Name: _____ Date: _____

Instructions: Use a check mark (✓) to indicate the items preferred.

Areas Of Interest

☐ Animals

   List preferred types: _____

☐ Weather	☐ Trucks	☐ Trains
☐ Dinosaurs	☐ Cars	☐ Science
☐ Math	☐ Numbers	☐ Shapes
☐ Machines	☐ Tools	☐ Clothes
☐ Outdoors	☐ Sports	☐ Computers

☐ List favorite TV programs: _____

☐ List favorite celebrities: _____

☐ List favorite colors: _____

☐ List favorite songs: _____

☐ List favorite places to go: _____

☐ Other: _____

☐ Other: _____

☐ Other: _____

Dislikes

☐ List foods disliked: _____

☐ List noises disliked: _____

☐ List activities disliked: _____

☐ List places does not like to go: _____

☐ List classroom materials disliked: _____

☐ List animals disliked: _____

☐ List any other dislikes: _____

_____

☐ List any known fears: _____

A Quick Word About Behavior/Reinforcement Plans

You can create a formal plan or an informal one: Simply, formal behavior plans usually involve some type of written program, even if brief. The program is spelled out or illustrated and essentially describes what the person earns as a result of his behavior. The plan may also highlight such items as cause/effect, contingencies and plans for what to do in a particular situation.

Informal plans are more like a deal. These plans are highly effective and work very well, especially during those in-the-moment situations. For instance, you could say, "If you do this, then you'll get this" or, "Once this happens, then you'll get this." The adult in charge is making a plan based on the situation and what she knows the other person wants. These informal reinforcement plans are the most common types of plans.

Section II

LEVEL 1: PLANNING FOR SUCCESS

Odd noises	Obstinent behaviors	Constant annoyance	Not listening	Refusing to follow directions
	Continually bothering others	Difficulty with calming down	Behavior does not look typical	

CHAPTER 4

Powerful Programming for Preschool, Elementary and Secondary School Children

PRESCHOOL CHILDREN

Everyone has heard the term *terrible twos* or *trying threes*. Working with young children can certainly be challenging at times, as they are trying to act on and begin to control parts of their environment. Young children's language is also developing rapidly, but they still are not adept at using verbal skills to communicate their feelings, wants or needs. Kids of this age group are very egocentric and are just learning how to interact with their peers on a very limited basis. When working with young children or those who have developmental delays who are displaying a variety of behaviors, it is important to remember the following:

- Everything a child does is behavior.
- Some behavior is purposeful and appropriate for meeting a child's needs.
- Some behavior occurs because a child is using all the strategies he has at that point in time to get his needs met.
- When a child uses a behavior that works to accomplish a goal, she will use that behavior again, and conversely, when that behavior doesn't work, she will try something different.

The most important thing to remember is that behavior is always communication. From the child's perspective, behavior is used to communicate a message when he has limited/no verbal language or when his language skills are not well developed. Sometimes, the behavior is a more efficient or effective way of getting his needs met. Additional factors that can affect behavior are:

- Age or developmental level
- Social skill level
- Learning style differences
- The physical environment
- . Sensory needs

Level 1 behaviors that are common for the preschool child are:

- Being crabby when tired or routine is changed
- Clinging to parent
- Not sharing
- Not responding to new adults
- Saying "no" to requests
- Pouting

ELEMENTARY SCHOOL CHILDREN

Elementary age children exist on a very wide spectrum, because we are working with children ages 5 to 11 with a multitude of developmental, emotional, physical and educational attributes. For this age group with Level 1 behaviors, we want to set up powerful programming pertaining to the larger group rather than to individuals. Components of powerful programming are:

- Rules and routines
- Parameters and expectations
- Schedules and procedures
- Whole-group reinforcement systems

SECONDARY SCHOOL CHILDREN (MIDDLE AND HIGH SCHOOL)

We believe that it is important to have behavior management systems that are age appropriate for kids at the secondary level. This includes plans for their ability level, the environment, motivations and approaches.

Rules and Routines

Good classroom management and large group management rely on rules and routines to be successful. Both adults and children need these rules and routines to thrive and learn.

Classroom rules should be simple, phrased positively and easy to understand and learn. For example, instead of saying "No hitting," we would say, "Keep your hands, feet and body to yourself."

Routines need to be taught and practiced just like any other skill. For example, kids need to learn how to get an adult's attention appropriately and what to do if they need an object.

Some examples of clear classroom rules are:

- Raise your hand if you want to talk.
- Keep your hands, feet, body and other objects to yourself.
- Use appropriate voice volume (see example).
- Line up in line/class order.
- Use kind words/language.
- Respect property.

Rules should be visually depicted, and with younger children, pictures are essential. Today's classrooms are filled with children with reading and language disorders as well as those for whom English is their second language. Thus, visually depicting rules is vital for understanding.

Some examples of routines that should be taught and practiced are:

- How to enter the room
- How to transition from individual to group areas
- Emergency routines
- How to leave the room in different situations
- Walking in the hallways
- Lunch/recess routines

Educators tend to practice these skills at the beginning of the year. However, it is important to practice these skills as the school year goes on. Don't forget that you need to continue to reinforce to allow kids to practice and learn these skills.

Parameters and Expectations

The most important reason to establish parameters and expectations is for consistency of behavioral responses for adults and children. Some examples of parameters and expectations are:

- Follow the rules/have established systems in place that outline specifics (written rules about behaviors and their consequences).
- Do your best: Have concrete examples that reward effort.
- Respect others: Teach and practice how to show respect.
- Ask for help: Teach who and when to ask for help.

Remember, people always think that rules are for children; however, the rules are for adults as well. Knowing the rules helps the adults react consistently to kids' behaviors. We all do better with parameters for how to behave in a certain circumstance. Rules create safety, and without this sense of security, other needs cannot be met.

Schedules and Procedures

As adults, we find ourselves referring to our planners and calendars frequently to schedule in our work and home activities. We refer to these schedules several times during the day to help guide us as we move from task to task. The same is true for elementary-age children as they navigate through their daily routines. Schedules can be used for the larger group, as well as for individual children.

DAILY SCHEDULE

1 ARRIVE AT SCHOOL

2 CHECK IN

3 READING

4 WRITING

5 MATH

6 RECESS

7 JOURNAL

8 PE/GYM

9 LUNCH

10 ART

11 MUSIC

12 BUS

Sample Schedule

Name: _____

Day: _____

	All Done
Put backpack in cubby	
Independent work	
Morning meeting	
Reading time	
Reading group	
Spelling work at desk	
Music class	
Speech	
Lunch	
Recess	
Special reading group	
Pack up backpack	
Go home	

CHAPTER 5
Group Reinforcement Strategies - 37 Interventions

People by nature are social beings. Groups of people certainly thrive in situations where the group feels reinforced through their behavior. Individual behavior is learned and shaped by the social influences with which the person is involved. The natural environment is a wonderful educator, and utilizing this idea is key. The power of whole-group reinforcement is amazing and should not be underestimated.

Some examples of whole-group reinforcement systems are:

- "Catching" someone being good
- Token economies (e.g., classroom points, bucks, marbles in a jar)
- Public praise
- Bringing in a special person
- Special group prize/privilege (e.g., popcorn day, extra recess)
- Contests
- Group getting to pick the reward (e.g., class votes on a movie)
- Having parents come to the class

LEVEL 1: SETTING THEM UP FOR SUCCESS

These ideas are meant to be used for groups and in environments in which we are trying to reinforce multiple individuals for the behaviors that we want to see.

Each intervention has indicators for which age group it is intended. However, with youth and different levels of ability, it might be necessary to use a different level even though they are in an older age bracket.

$\mathbf{P}$ = Preschool age (typically ages 3-5)

$\mathbf{E}$ = Elementary age (typically ages 5-11)

$\mathbf{M}$ = Middle school age (typically ages 12-14)

$\mathbf{H}$ = High school age (typically ages 14-18)

Level 1– Group Reinforcers
Intervention Activities

"Cool Clips": Earn one clip for a specific behavior or combination of behaviors (e.g., lining up quietly, raising your hand). When a specified number of clips are earned, the class earns a reinforcement. **E, M**

Ticket Trade: Tickets are given out for a specific behavior or combination of behaviors. Tickets can be color coded and/or have a point value assigned. Tickets can be given out individually, for small groups or for a larger group. Tickets can represent privileges, buying power, reinforcement choice and even an indicator on a level system. **E, M, H**

Keys on a Ring: The teacher has either old keys or colored keys from the hardware store in her pocket along with a key ring. When the teacher notices a specific behavior or combination of prosocial behaviors, she puts a key on the ring. When the key ring is full (or a specified amount is reached), the class receives a reinforcer. **P, E**

P = Preschool age   **E** = Elementary age   **M** = Middle school age   **H** = High school age

Complete the Calendar: Place a blank month calendar in the front of the room. Put the numbers for the days of the month in an envelope or container. When you "catch a student being good," have the child (or the adult in charge) draw a number and place it on the calendar. When the calendar is filled up, the class earns the reinforcer. **P, E, M**

Mon	Tues	Wed	Thur	Fri	Sat	Sun
			1	2	3	4	5
6	7	8	9	10	11	12
13	14	15	16	17	18	19
20	21	22	23	24	25	25
26	27	28	29	30		

Puzzle: Put a photo or drawing of something the class is working toward (e.g., a toy, a bucket of popcorn, the phrase "extra recess") and draw puzzle piece borders on the picture. Cut the picture into puzzle pieces. Students earn pieces for appropriate behavior. When the puzzle is complete, the students earn the reinforcer on the puzzle. **P, E, M**

Spell the Prize: Choose a reinforcer (e.g., person, activity, toy, movie title) and cut out letters that spell out its name. Kids earn a letter when they display a specified behavior. When the name of the reinforcer is spelled out, the kids earn the named reinforcer. **E, M**

HARRY   MUMMY
harry   mummy
DADDY   LION
daddy   lion
TRAIN   MILK
train   milk

P = Preschool age   **E** = Elementary age   **M** = Middle school age   **H** = High school age

Scoops: Draw a picture of an ice cream cone and decide on a certain number of scoops that need to be earned to get a reinforcer. When students display appropriate behavior, they earn a scoop. When all the scoops are on top of the cone, the students earn the reinforcer. **P, E**

X Games: Children earn picture parts of a bike, trike, roller blades, skateboard, etc. When they have earned all the necessary parts, they can earn time for a bike ride, roller blade session, etc. **P, E**

Show Me the Money: Students earn play money for exhibiting appropriate behaviors, completing work, etc. Students can use the money to purchase items from a school store (e.g., snacks, drinks, toys) or can save the money to purchase a larger reinforcer (e.g., game day, field trip). **P, E, M, H**

P = Preschool age   **E** = Elementary age   **M** = Middle school age   **H** = High school age

Project Ziploc®: Kids can earn time to complete a cooking or art project. The kids earn individual pieces necessary for the project (e.g., measuring cup, ingredients, spoons, bowls for a cooking project). You can put the items in a Ziploc baggie as the kids earn them. When all the pieces are earned, then the kids are able to participate in the project. **P, E, M, H**

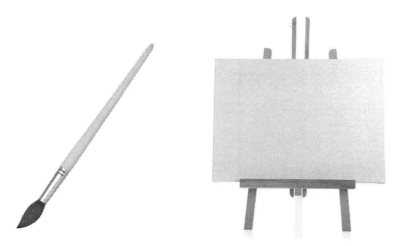

Pizza/Taco/Sandwich/Sweet Treat Party: Pictures/photos of the individual items needed are earned for exhibiting appropriate individual or group behavior (e.g., quiet when teacher talks, hands to self in line). When all the necessary items are earned, then the class gets the party. Some examples are:
- Earn pictures of slices of pizza and then add a specific amount of toppings. When all ingredients are earned, then the class gets a pizza.
- Earn pictures of the ingredients needed for tacos (e.g., a specific number of shells, cheese, meat, lettuce, tomato, sauce). When all ingredients are earned, then the class gets tacos.
- Create a large paper cookie. Students get to add pictures of M&Ms to it. When a specified amount of candies are on the cookie, the class gets a sweet treat.
- Get a popcorn box or a picture of one. Students earn pieces (e.g., pictures or sponges cut up into popcorn shapes). When the container is filled, then the class earns a popcorn party. **P, E, M**

| P = Preschool age | E = Elementary age | M = Middle school age | H = High school age |

Snow Cone Freeze: Get a picture of a real bucket. Place pictures of snowballs on the picture bucket or paper snowballs in the real bucket when children display appropriate behaviors. When the bucket is filled or the children have earned a specified amount of "snow," have a snow cone party. **P, E, M**

Tree Trimming: Depending on the season of the year, have students earn green or colored leaves for demonstrating pro-social behaviors (e.g., giving compliments, saying thank you, waiting their turn). When the tree is filled with leaves, then the group earns a reinforcer (perhaps a walk to the park). Alternatives include replacing green leaves with fall-colored leaves, making fall-colored leaves fall off the tree, putting buds on an empty tree and having leaves replace buds on a tree. You get the idea! **P, E**

Linked In: Use toy links to make a strand of a specified amount. Kids earn the links by using the appropriate behaviors of your choice. When the strand of links is complete, the group earns a reinforcer. **P, E**

P = Preschool age   **E** = Elementary age   **M** = Middle school age   **H** = High school age

We Can Build a Snowman: Fill up a picture of a snowman's body with cotton balls and add a hat, scarf, nose, eyes, etc. when children display specific behaviors or a combination of behaviors. When the snowman is complete, a reinforcer is in order. **P, E**

Book Benefits: Put up a bookmark for each book read by the students. When a certain number of books are read, then the students earn a reinforcer. **E**

Compliment Crazy: Catch kids giving compliments and put a marble in the jar. When the jar is filled up, compliment the kids on their behavior and have a game day or give another reinforcer. **E, M**

P = Preschool age   **E** = Elementary age   **M** = Middle school age   **H** = High school age

Green Thumb (Greenhouse/Gardening Projects): The opportunity to do this project can be based on earning the privilege, or it can be an automatic privilege as part of the overall curriculum/program. Have kids help with planting and caring for different types of flowers, plants and vegetables. Some minor landscaping can be done as well. Assign different subtasks within the overall job to give the kids a sense of responsibility. **M, H**

Recycling Squad: Children can earn the chance to help with recycling tasks as a contribution to their school/community, etc. Some programs also allow for earning points, dollars, etc., and so the act of recycling can be reinforcing on a couple of levels. **M, H**

Teacher Assistant/Staff Assistant: If a kid earns the privilege, he gets to be the helper. This serves several functions: Attention, acceptance, escape and control needs are all met through this privilege. **E, M, H**

P = Preschool age   **E** = Elementary age   **M** = Middle school age   **H** = High school age

Go for the Gold (Watching Sports/Activity Videos): Students earn the privilege of watching part of a recent football game, baseball game, art extravaganza, concert, etc., on video with an adult. Having a mutual interest also helps make a connection and provides a nice escape from the grind of daily activities. **M, H**

Early OUT: This gives kids a chance to leave for lunch early or get out of a task early based on their behavior. Early OUT! works great with kids when they have been working on challenging tasks or they have been corrected a certain behavior. Getting to leave early is motivating for many people! **M, H**

Sell It: Organize a group of children to make/produce items to sell. This could be done as a fundraising event, which is even more fun. Incorporate planning, organization, record keeping, supply, inventory and accounting into this activity to help teach these skills. To assist with behavior, set a requirement for behavioral expectations to make the activity is a privilege rather than a chore. **M, H**

P = Preschool age   **E** = Elementary age   **M** = Middle school age   **H** = High school age

The Hunter Games: This is essentially an earned scavenger hunt. At either random or assigned times, based on positive behaviors, assign kids certain items, people or places to find and send them on missions. This can be done in multiple settings and is great for those kids that need to be up and moving. **M, H**

Tunes Time! Getting to listen to music can be reinforcing for many people. It is fairly easy to use different devices to allow this to happen. There are several ways to use this reinforcement in some fun and interesting ways:

- The group can listen to music, and the person with the most points gets to choose the music.
- The adult gets to choose the music if the students do not earn enough points. There is a friendly competitive factor with this variation, as the students probably will not want to listen to the music the adult likes.
- Students in different small groups can listen to different music. For instance, one group may listen to rap while another listens to country.
- Have the student of the day choose the radio station/music.
- Students earn tickets or some other points, and each time there is a new point leader, that person gets to pick the music.
- Use certain songs for certain tasks: This is really helpful for younger children (e.g., clean-up song, line-up song).

Note: There are great benefits to having music on as background noise and simply to help students relax. **P, E, M, H**

P = Preschool age   E = Elementary age   M = Middle school age   H = High school age

Phone Fun: Allowing kids to use their phones at appropriate times is typically going to be a big win. In most cases, kids are not allowed to use phones in a classroom or treatment environment and for good reason. However, building this time in as reinforcement can have a huge impact on positive behavior development and continuance. Of course, with the phones comes the ability to text, so that will need to be taken into consideration based on the circumstance. **M, H**

Awesome Foods: There are so many fun ways to use food as motivation and as reinforcement. (Never use food as a punishment.) There are many fun ways to use food to increase positive behavior, minimize and even eliminate negative behavior and increase academic and therapeutic work/activities:

- Have snacks available in the classroom that are not based on earning rewards: Everyone gets the snack. This is our favorite and creates an atmosphere of caring and teamwork.
- Have the students pick the food they will earn as a group after a big event like a test, project or completion of a piece of therapeutic work.
- The student with the highest points for the week gets to pick the snacks.
- Have the students develop a menu along with the price of each item in terms of points or tickets. Then, based on what they have earned and have in their ticket bank, they can purchase those snacks from the menu.
- Dole out different snacks and then have snack trade time. Students can trade snacks with anyone else in the room and can continue trading until they get the one they like best.
- Play UNO® for snacks. Each Draw 2 or Draw 4 gets you 2 or 4 additional snack pieces. The winner of the game gets the remaining snacks.
- Bring in a pizza/cookies/tacos, etc., on a day when you know the activity is going to be more challenging.
- Have fruit, healthy snack items, etc., available in a basket or dish for students whenever they want.

Note: We all need food, and for some young people, not getting food is a huge part of their lives. By providing food/snacks, we are creating a common link with young people but also communicating that we are compassionate and care about them. Also, food helps regulate blood sugar and keeps up the energy levels. **P, E, M, H**

P = Preschool age   **E** = Elementary age   **M** = Middle school age   **H** = High school age

Beverage Brigade: First of all, we believe that kids should have continued/easy access to water at all times. Simply letting kids have a water bottle at their desk or on their person prevents them leaving the area to get a drink and also prevents dehydration, the leading cause of headaches.

- Use the point system to allow kids to earn a soda/fruit drink after accumulating a certain number of points.
- Surprise a class with their beverage of choice and have it available for the kids at a break.
- Investing in a purified water dispenser is a great use of money, and many dispensers also provide hot water to make tea, etc. **P, E, M, H**

Get OUT of Here: Let the students go outside after earning a break through good behavior. Give them a certain amount of time to just talk, socialize and hang out. These little breaks do take time, but work time is increased when behavior problems are reduced. Think about the amount of time saved in overall behavior management! **P, E, M, H**

P = Preschool age   **E** = Elementary age   **M** = Middle school age   **H** = High school age

Halvsies (Work Reduction Program): Establish steps for how kids can end up doing less work on a certain task or set of tasks! For instance, if a kid exhibits a certain amount of good behavior, then she only has to do half of an assignment. This is a really fun way to engage kids that will actually increase their productivity because although they are doing less, they may be working harder on what they are doing. **E, M, H**

No More Homework: The benefits of homework can be debated anyway. Use no homework as a reinforcement: When students exhibit a particular behavior, they are excused from a homework assignment. Or, you can require students to reach a certain level or number of good behaviors to earn no homework. For instance, "If you are compliant and follow directions the first time during this lesson, you will have no homework." See how much behavior improves by not having homework for that day. **E, M, H**

P = Preschool age   **E** = Elementary age   **M** = Middle school age   **H** = High school age

Chatter Box: Choose some topics pertinent to the age group with which you are working. Have the students select which topic they want to cover and then engage them in a conversation about it for a set amount of time. This also works in a group treatment setting. The important thing here is to get the kids talking about anything: Communicating is a social skill that is learned like anything else, and so practice is important. Plus, it builds connections to the adult(s) in charge beyond the topic/lesson of that moment. **E, M, H**

Guaranteed Success: Example: "Everyone has an A on this quiz—all you have to do is look at it!" Or, "All of you have 100% on this test: Now, do the best you can answering all the questions." Or, "Everyone write your name, favorite food and hobby on a sheet of paper, and you will have an A." This sets the stage for success and takes away the fear of failing. **E, M, H**

| P = Preschool age | E = Elementary age | M = Middle school age | H = High school age |

Take Control: Allow children to take some control of their environment: Let them choose a seating arrangement, decide whether there is background music, choose the order of activities to be done that day, etc. **E, M, H**

Switch Up: Changing up the schedule can be done in a lot of fun ways. The assigned activities will still get done, but the kids get to control choosing how those activities get done:

- Backwards Class: Start with the last thing, like recess, and end with the warm up or ice breaker.
- "Roll the Dice" Schedule: Number each item to be done in the setting from 1 to 6. A participant rolls a die, and whatever number comes up determines the item that is completed.
- Mixed up Schedule: List all of the things to be done, and then have participants pick which ones to do.
- Slap Jack Activity: Play Slap Jack, and whoever gets the jack gets to pick the activity.

Note: Remember, the adult is in charge of the overall schedule, but the kids are getting some control by choosing how the activities are done. **E, M, H**

P = Preschool age   **E** = Elementary age   **M** = Middle school age   **H** = High school age

Presentation Picks: Anything that reduces anxiety is reinforcing. For example, a student is anxious about speaking to the group: Allow him to choose his output source: Poster board display, presentation, report, video, etc. **P, E, M, H**

Juggling Jobs: Break a big task down into smaller tasks so that everyone involved takes a very small part. This gets all the kids involved and makes big tasks seem much more manageable. **E, M, H**

P = Preschool age   **E** = Elementary age   **M** = Middle school age   **H** = High school age

Section III

LEVEL 2: REINFORCEMENT FOR GOOD BEHAVIORS

Getting in trouble (school, daycare, etc)	Outright defiance	Temper tantrums	Lack of success	Doing things on purpose to cause problems
	Arguing	Starting Fight	Violating rules	Danger of moving to Level 3

CHAPTER 6

Reinforcement Plans Based on Motivation

If after utilizing Level 1 strategies you still have a child who is exhibiting behaviors that are causing problems in your environment, then it's time to move to Level 2 strategies. You will take a systematic approach with your child when designing programs that will reduce inappropriate behaviors and establish prosocial replacement behaviors.

ASSESSMENT

Instead of using a trial-and-error approach, you will have much greater success and a quicker turnaround if you use some assessment tools. Chapter 2 contains general facts, several assessment tools and necessary forms to gather information. Gathering information about the child, the behavior of concern and environmental, learning and social factors is the first step in a systematic assessment.

LOOKING AT DATA/ASSESSMENT INFORMATION

After gathering information, the next step is to amass the data and assessment information into a plan to help the child with her behaviors. This compilation of information will allow the adult to identify the function of the child's behavior and what extraneous factors affect it. We walk you through an approach that considers motivational schemes, behavior plan formation, reinforcement ideas for the individual child and how to teach replacement skills for the inappropriate behaviors.

Remember that this level includes assessment and reviewing your data to develop programming that is appropriate and fits the needs/motivation of individuals.

For the information on assessments and motivation schemes, refer back to the earlier sections. Refer back to information gathered to develop interventions found at this level for the children and youth with whom you are working.

After accessing information using the *Assessment of Motivation Tool (AMS)*, it will be much easier to match the motivation with a reinforcement program for that individual. The next set of reinforcement ideas matches with a type of motivation. Each type of motivation will be followed with ideas for possible behavior management/reinforcement systems. For instance, if a child is motivated by a token economy, then the following ideas might be a good start:

- Earn a token, coins, etc. for each positive behavior demonstrated.
- Earn tickets/paper money, etc. for positive behaviors.
- Earn other tangible items in a container (e.g., marbles in a jar).

The following is a review list of the motivation schemes found in the *AMS*. These will be very important in developing individual reinforcement plans and for teaching new skills. Again, don't forget all those fun Level 1 ideas!

BEHAVIOR PLANS

A behavior plan can exist in almost any setting. The plan can be formal with detailed areas to monitor and track, or it can be very informal, almost like making a "deal" with the kid. Typically, behavior plans should be more detailed when the behavior is more severe and if there are several other people involved that might help in monitoring the plan. There is a strong preference in individual work for the behavior plan to be more informal. The informal behavior plan can exist because of the relationship between the adult and young person. The relationship is paramount in terms of working with children and youth with behavioral issues. Some ideas about behavior plans include the following:

- Why would somebody want to follow the plan?
- Have we defined the behaviors and defined the purpose of the behavior?
- What will be the incentive for behavior improvement?
- Is there an understanding about the motivation that this person has?

A behavior plan essentially exists in this paradigm: "If you do this, then I'll do this." Or, "If you do these things, then you'll get these things." Essentially, a behavior plan is just a deal between parties.

It is very important to match the behavior plan to the person's motivation(s). For example, if the person is motivated by having time with an adult (social/emotional, attention) then the behavior plan should have a clear way for her to earn that time.

Following is a review of the motivation schemes covered earlier in the book, including an idea for a behavior plan. This is not an exhaustive list by any means but rather a way for you to think about a behavior plan for a particular situation. Whether the behavior plans are formal (written out with monitoring systems in place) or informal (an agreement between adult and child/youth) is up to you and/or the environment in which you are working.

Motivation and Behavior Plan Suggestion

- **Extrinsic:** The plan should highlight the thing that the kid is getting. In other words, how does he earn the item? You might also want to think about short term versus long term. Sometimes it is helpful to have items earned very immediately, with bigger items earned for a series of behaviors.

- **Intrinsic:** The plan is going to give the kid a sense of pride or the feeling of accomplishment and/or confidence. This might be displayed visually, using pictures/words to aid in comprehension, but verbal recognition may have just as powerful impact.

- **Social/Emotional:** Simply put, the plan will help the kid get her social and emotional needs met to the best of your ability. Perhaps the plan in place helps her by allowing her time with her peers? Or, perhaps the plan allows her time to get one-on-one time with someone special?

- **Attention:** The plan helps the child gain attention from the person/persons from whom he wants attention. Perhaps he gains attention from the adults in his life or gets attention from peers. The plan needs to provide him some way of gaining positive attention for his accomplishments.

- **Fear:** The plan helps the child avoid or perhaps mitigate the fear she might have about something. For example, after a student takes the first few steps in preparing her speech, the plan allows her to give the speech via video to quell her fear about public speaking.

- **Sensory:** These plans have built-in sensory time that can also be fun and great diversions. Some activity can be earned, while other activities are simply built in as part of the schedule.

- **Escape:** Escape-oriented plans have built-in time that allows the kid to escape appropriately during different parts of the day. For instance, if a student is working off of a structured schedule and he completes his tasks, he earns time getting to do a preferred task.

- **Control:** Control-based plans give the child actual control or at least the perception of control. For instance, plans in which the child chooses assigned activities and then chooses the reinforcement gives her the perception of control even though everything is assigned to her.

- **Pain:** This type of plan helps someone deal with the type of pain he is in or might be in. A basic treatment plan to help someone with his depression might fit this type of plan. Essentially, by following the plan, the kid can feel less pain.

Of course, one must take into account that there is a lot of overlap between motivations. Fortunately, what helps with one particular type of motivation can often help with another.

SELF-ASSESSMENT

Think about yourself for a minute. What motivates you? If you were writing a behavior plan for yourself, how would you want it to look? What would be the best way to get you to change your behavior?

This exercise can be helpful because it helps us relate to others better. Since we are trying to change another person's behavior, it is important to realize what it takes for us to change our own behavior. We will be more sensitive to the needs of the children for whom we are developing behavior plans if we consider how we might feel about the plan if it was put in place for us.

Please go through this list and simply mark yes or no if the motivation listed is something that applies to you. You can also do this on a separate sheet of paper so multiple people can do the same exercise. Where you mark "yes" is going to be an indication that you prefer that idea in terms of motivation.

Intrinsic-Internal Motivation Types

- A sense of mastery?
- Realization of an accomplishment?
- A sense of satisfaction?
- Self-achievement, thus confidence?
- Receiving praise or acknowledgement?
- Helping others and feeling good about it?

Extrinsic-External Motivation Types

- Token economies?
- Stickers, good marks, etc.?
- Behavioral charts?
- Trophies, stripes, badges, etc.?
- Money or other material items?

Social/Emotional

- Belonging to a peer group?
- Being cared for/feeling loved and appreciated?
- Belonging to a community, group, society, etc.?
- Feeling safe, attached/bonded with caregivers?
- Having friends, pleasant social contacts?

Attention

- Being recognized as an important person?
- Being noticed for behavior?
- Receiving acknowledgements (praise, etc.)?
- Recognition of personal attributes?

Control

- Control over one's environment?
- Control over routine and/or schedule?
- Power over decisions?
- The ability to make choices?
- Control over emotions?
- Controls reactions to emotional situations?

Sensory

- Getting physical needs met?
- Having hearing levels increased or reduced?
- Visual adjustments?
- Avoiding or acquiring pleasant smells?
- Eating desired foods/avoiding undesired foods?

Pain

- Avoiding pain altogether?
- Getting assistance when in physical pain?
- Assistance with medication, adjustments, etc.?
- Appropriate care for emotional pain?

Fear

- Avoiding a fear entirely?
- Mitigating a fear?
- Developing coping skills for fears?
- Accommodating for real or imagined fears?

Escape

- Getting satisfaction from leaving environments?
- Escaping from tasks due to perceived incompetence?
- Leaving environment due to confusion?
- Leaving to gain control or attention?

CHAPTER 7

Individual Reinforcement Strategies - 31 Interventions

GUIDE TO MATCHING MOTIVATION SCHEMES TO A REINFORCEMENT PLAN

In the following section is a list of ideas for reinforcement plans. Each reinforcement idea is followed by a letter code to help you identify the type of motivation that goes with the reinforcement idea.

Following are several examples for methods to use different reinforcement plans. Certainly, you can take these ideas and alter them to fit your particular situation or, you can just implement them exactly as illustrated.

Use the motivation scheme coding to help match the reinforcement plan to the child's actual motivation. While a perfect match might not always be easy to find, you should be able to get fairly close to matching motivation with a plan.

Finally, it is important to remember to not get to set in one plan. Meaning, being flexible is often a key ingredient in working with challenging kids. So, start with one plan and then if you need to, move on to another plan that fits the motivation or a new motivation as interests can change.

I = Intrinsic/Internal

E = Extrinsic/External

S/E = Social/Emotional

A = Attention

C = Control

S = Sensory

P = Pain

F = Fear

Esc = Escape

Level – 2 Individual Reinforcers
Intervention Activities

Spell Out Phone Numbers: A student earns individual numerals to complete a phone number (e.g., time/temp, parent) when displaying a specified behavior. When the student has all the numerals in the phone number, he is able to complete the phone call. **I, A, C**

TV Show and Characters: Some kids are really tied into their favorite television shows and movies and the characters in them. There are a variety of things you can do with reinforcers that tie in to kid's favorite TV shows, movies and characters. Some examples are

- Watching video clips of the show after earning viewing minutes for demonstrating specific behaviors.
- Playing with a stuffed animal character from the show/movie. Set a timer so that the student knows when to give the stuffed animal back.
- Purchasing or making your own game board with the favorite characters. The kid can play the game after earning the opportunity through demonstration of specific behaviors.
- Kids can also earn the chance to look at books or magazines about their favorite show or characters.
- Young kids might enjoy the opportunity to earn time to role-play with toys from their favorite show.
- Kids might also like to earn stickers of their favorite characters.
- Older kids can act as a movie critic and share their opinions orally or in writing.
- Some kids may want to create their own storyboard about the movie. **I, E, C**

I = Intrinsic/Internal   **E** = Extrinsic/External   **S/E** = Social/Emotional
A = Attention   **C** = Control   **S** = Sensory   **P** = Pain   **F** = Fear   **Esc** = Escape

Action Heroes Action: Action heroes can be big-time reinforcers for some children. Some ways you can individually reinforce a child using the action hero theme include

- Earning time to read/look at books about the hero.
- Having dress-up items that the child can wear for a specific amount of time.
- Earning stickers with the action heroes on them.
- Watching video clips for a specific amount of time after the child has earned them for exhibiting identified behaviors.
- Utilizing comic strip apps for a specified time when the child has earned them for exhibiting identified behaviors. **I, E, C**

House of Cards: There are lots of different card games that many kids enjoy playing, such as Pokémon®, UNO®, War, Go Fish and Spoons. Adults can use these card activities to increase positive behaviors in individual students.

- Kids can purchase cards, such as Pokémon, in the school/class store after earning "money" by showing positive behaviors.
- Kids can earn time at lunch to play cards with a friend.
- A kid can earn time to instruct others how to play a specific card game.
- Kids can earn time to build card houses.
- Kids can earn individual or several cards for specific behaviors. When they have earned the entire deck, they can play card games during a specified time. **S/E, A, C**

I = Intrinsic/Internal   **E** = Extrinsic/External   **S/E** = Social/Emotional
A = Attention   **C** = Control   **S** = Sensory   **P** = Pain   **F** = Fear   **Esc** = Escape

Beauty Time: A student can earn items for a doll or for herself to use on hair (e.g., barrettes, comb, hair ties). She can also earn items for nail care, such as nail polish, nail stickers and a nail brush. These items can be placed in a bag/container as the student earns each item for displaying specific behaviors. **I, E, S/E, A, C, S**

Animal Acts: Many children love animals, and there are several different ways you can utilize an animal theme to reinforce individual kids.

- Animal stickers can be earned for exhibiting a behavior. Example: When you raise your hand five times instead of blurting out, you earn a lion sticker.
- A student can earn time with a therapy dog or school/classroom pet. Students can also feed a classroom pet or fish.
- For a reading/writing project, an individual student can complete the project on his favorite animal. Students are more apt to complete work when it is on a preferred subject.
- A student can earn animal puppets for demonstrating specific behaviors. When they have earned several puppets, they can have time to play with the puppets and even put on a puppet show. Students can also make their own puppets with socks, pipe cleaners, buttons, etc.
- A child might like to earn time with a stuffed animal for exhibiting positive behaviors to replace negative behaviors.
- There are many video sites/computer activities that include animals. A student can earn time to watch/ interact with these sites after she has demonstrated targeted behaviors. **E, S/E, A, S, Esc**

I = Intrinsic/Internal   **E** = Extrinsic/External   **S/E** = Social/Emotional
A = Attention   **C** = Control   **S** = Sensory   **P** = Pain   **F** = Fear   **Esc** = Escape

Zoom, Zoom: Many kids like cars. For younger kids, they like playing with small cars and trucks. Older kids like to complete car models or look at car magazines. Some reinforcers that you could use with a student who has an interest in cars are

- A kid could earn a small car or truck that is placed into a baggie whenever he demonstrates a targeted behavior (hands down while lining up, for example). At the end of the day, the kid can have time to play with the cars in the baggie.
- A kid can earn a coloring book page after showing she can complete a math worksheet, for example.
- A kid can earn time to look at a car magazine or book.
- Younger kids could earn car stickers for exhibiting positive behaviors.
- A kid could buy a car model with "funny money" that was earned by accumulating dollars through demonstration of targeted positive behaviors. **E, Esc**

Sport Surprises: Students are often involved in sports either as participants or spectators. Some activities that you could try using sports as a reinforcer are

- Students can earn sport cards with famous athletes on them.
- Students can earn time to look at a sports magazine or time to read a book about a certain sport or athlete.
- Students can do reading/writing assignments using their favorite sport or athlete as the topic.
- Students can earn time to talk about any sport contest they want.
- A student can earn a trip to visit the local university or professional team to meet players, observe training, etc. The student would have to earn points by using targeted replacement behaviors. **I, E, A, C, Esc**

I = Intrinsic/Internal   **E** = Extrinsic/External   **S/E** = Social/Emotional
A = Attention   **C** = Control   **S** = Sensory   **P** = Pain   **F** = Fear   **Esc** = Escape

Visual Reinforcement Plans: Many reinforcement plans are more effective when the child can "see" how much further he has to go before earning the reinforcer. It is easy to take any reinforcing activity and make it visual for the child. The following pages have some examples. **E, can lead into other motivations**

A. Using a picture or worksheet with squares (see below), you fill in the squares when a child exhibits a specific behavior(s). You can even write those behaviors on the sheet so all staff can see it and reinforce the child. When the boxes are filled up then for example, the child can spend 10 minutes with the school's therapy dog.

B. Using a picture of a school of fish, the child can cross off an individual fish when displaying a positive behavior. When the fish are all marked off, then the child can feed the fish, look at the fish in the aquarium, go outside to the school pond to watch/feed the fish, watch a 10-minute video on fish, look at a fish book, play a fish-related computer game, etc.

C. When a child completes a task or uses a specified prosocial behavior, an adult can circle the picture of a CD/DVD. When all the CD/DVD pictures are circled, then the child can spend 10 minutes playing a preferred computer game.

D. Having children use replacement skills (e.g., using your words) is always a goal for instructors/ parents. Adults can specify some of the prosocial statements they want the child to use. When the child uses the appropriate statement three times, then she gets to engage in a preferred activity for a specified amount of time.

A.

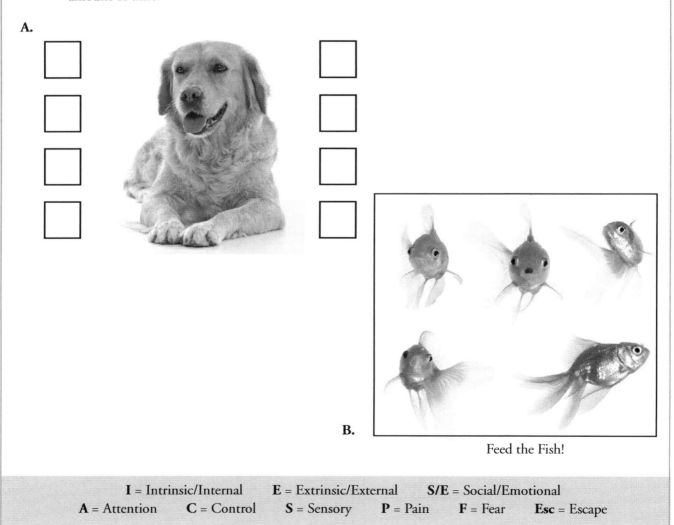

B.

Feed the Fish!

C.

Select or Name Your Computer Game: _____

D.

Use Your Words:

1. _____

2. _____

3. _____

4. _____

1	2	3

I = Intrinsic/Internal   **E** = Extrinsic/External   **S/E** = Social/Emotional

A = Attention   **C** = Control   **S** = Sensory   **P** = Pain   **F** = Fear   **Esc** = Escape

"Cool Clips": Earn one clip for a specific behavior or combination of behaviors (e.g., lining up quietly, raising your hand). When a specified amount is earned, the student earns a reinforcer. **E**

Ticket Trade: Tickets are given out for a specific behavior or combination of behaviors. Tickets can be color coded and/or have point value assigned. They can be given out individually, for small groups or for a larger group. Tickets can represent privileges, buying power, reinforcement choice and even an indicator on a level system. **E, C**

Keys on a Ring: The teacher has either old keys or colored keys from the hardware store, in his pocket along with a key ring. When the teacher notices a specific behavior or combination of prosocial behaviors, he puts a key on the ring. When the key ring is full (or a specified amount is reached), the student receives a reinforcer. **E**

I = Intrinsic/Internal   **E** = Extrinsic/External   **S/E** = Social/Emotional
A = Attention   **C** = Control   **S** = Sensory   **P** = Pain   **F** = Fear   **Esc** = Escape

Puzzle Reinforcers: Take a picture or a photo of what the child is working toward (e.g., a toy, a bucket of popcorn, the phrase "extra recess") and draw puzzle piece borders on the photo/picture. Cut it up into puzzle pieces, and then the child earns pieces for appropriate behavior. When the puzzle is complete, the child earns the reinforcer on the puzzle. **E, A**

Spell The Prize: Choose a reinforcer (e.g., person, activity, toy, movie name) and cut out letters that spell its name. The student earns a letter when she displays a specified behavior. When the name of the reinforcer is spelled out, the student earns that reinforcer. **E, A**

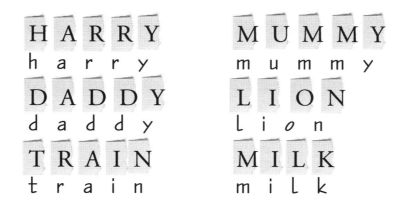

HARRY	MUMMY
harry	mummy
DADDY	LION
daddy	lion
TRAIN	MILK
train	milk

I = Intrinsic/Internal   **E** = Extrinsic/External   **S/E** = Social/Emotional
A = Attention   **C** = Control   **S** = Sensory   **P** = Pain   **F** = Fear   **Esc** = Escape

X Games: A kid earns picture parts of a bike, trike, roller blades, skateboard, etc. When he has earned all the necessary parts, the kid gets time for the activity depicted. **E, Esc, S, C**

Show Me the Money: A student earns play money for exhibiting appropriate behaviors, completing work, etc. She can use the money to purchase items from a school store (e.g., snacks, drinks, toys) or save money to purchase a larger reinforcer (e.g., game day, field trip). **E**

Project Ziploc: A student can earn time to complete a cooking or art project. He earns individual pieces necessary for the project (e.g., the measuring cup, ingredients, spoons, bowls for a cooking project). You can put the items in a Ziploc® baggie as the student earns them. When all the pieces are earned, then the student is able to participate in the project. **E, C**

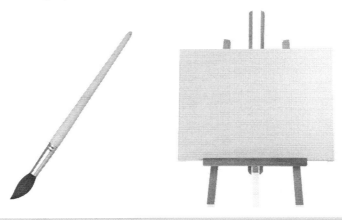

I = Intrinsic/Internal **E** = Extrinsic/External **S/E** = Social/Emotional
A = Attention **C** = Control **S** = Sensory **P** = Pain **F** = Fear **Esc** = Escape

Linked In: Use toy links to make a strand of a specified amount. A child earns the links by using appropriate behaviors of your choice. When the strand of links is complete, the child earns a reinforcer. **E**

Green Thumb: The opportunity to do this project can be based on earning the privilege, or it can be an automatic privilege as part of the overall curriculum/program. Have a kid help with planting and caring for different types of flowers, plants, vegetables, etc. Some minor landscaping can be done as well. Assign different subtasks within the overall job to give the kid a sense of responsibility. **I, S, S/E, C, Esc**

Recycling Squad: A student can earn the chance to help with recycling tasks as a contribution to their school/community, etc. Some programs also allow for earning points, dollars, etc., and so the act of recycling can be reinforcing on a couple of levels. **Esc, S, I**

I = Intrinsic/Internal   E = Extrinsic/External   S/E = Social/Emotional
A = Attention   C = Control   S = Sensory   P = Pain   F = Fear   Esc = Escape

Teacher Assistant/Staff Assistant: If a child earns the privilege, she gets to be the helper. This serves several functions: Attention, acceptance, escape and control needs are all met through this privilege. **I, S/E, A, C, Esc**

Go for the Gold (Watching Sports/Activity Videos): Earn the privilege of watching part of a recent football game, baseball game, art extravaganza, concert, etc., on video with an adult. Having a mutual interest helps make a connection and provides a nice escape from the grind of daily activities. **Esc**

Early OUT: This gives a kid a chance to leave for lunch early or get out of a task early based on his behavior. Early OUT works great with kids when they have been working on challenging tasks or they have corrected a certain behavior. Getting to leave early is motivating for many people! **Esc, C**

I = Intrinsic/Internal   E = Extrinsic/External   S/E = Social/Emotional
A = Attention   C = Control   S = Sensory   P = Pain   F = Fear   Esc = Escape

Tunes Time: Getting to listen to music can be reinforcing for many people. It is fairly easy to use different devices for this. There are several ways to use this reinforcement in some fun and interesting ways with individuals as well as with a group:

- The group can listen to music, and the child with the most points gets to choose.
- The adult gets to choose the music if the children do not earn enough points. There is friendly competitive factor using this, as the children probably will not want to listen to the music the adult likes.
- Children in different small groups can listen to different music. For instance, one group listens to rap in one group, another to country, etc.
- Have the child of the day choose the radio station/music.
- Using the ticket system or some other point system, each time there is a new point leader, that person gets to pick the music.
- Use certain songs for certain tasks: This is really helpful for younger children (e.g., clean-up song, line-up song).

Note: There are great benefits to having music on as background noise and simply to get people to relax.

S, Esc, I

Awesome Foods: There are so many fun ways to use food as motivation and as reinforcement. (Never use food as a punishment.) There are many fun ways to use food to increase positive behavior, minimize and even eliminate negative behavior and increase academic and therapeutic work/activities:

- Have snacks available in the classroom that are not based on earning rewards: Everyone gets the snack. This is our favorite and creates an atmosphere of caring and teamwork.
- Have the students pick the food they will earn as a group after a big event like a test, project or \ completion of a piece of therapeutic work.
- The student with the highest points for the week gets to pick the snacks.
- Have the students develop a menu along with the price of each item in terms of points or tickets. Then, based on what they have earned and have in their ticket bank, they can purchase those snacks from the menu.
- Dole out different snacks and then have snack trade time. Students can trade snacks with anyone in the room and continue trading until they get the one they like best.

I = Intrinsic/Internal	E = Extrinsic/External	S/E = Social/Emotional		
A = Attention	C = Control	S = Sensory	P = Pain	F = Fear	Esc = Escape

- Play UNO for snacks. Each Draw 2 or Draw 4 gets you 2 or 4 additional snack pieces. The winner of the game gets the remaining snacks.
- Bring in a pizza/cookies/tacos, etc., on a day when you know the activity is going to be more challenging.
- Have fruit, healthy snack items, etc., available in a basket or dish for students whenever they want.

Note: We all need food, and for some young people, not getting food is a huge part of their lives. By providing food/snacks, we are creating a common link with young people but also communicating that we are compassionate and care about them. Also, food helps regulate blood sugar and keeps up the energy levels. **I, S, S/E**

Beverage Brigade: First of all, we believe that kids should have continued/easy access to water at all times. Simply letting kids have a water bottle at their desk or on their person prevents them having to leave the area to get a drink and also prevents dehydration, the leading cause of headaches. Some of these ideas can be used with individuals or with a group.
- Use the point system to allow a kid to earn a soda/fruit drink after accumulating so many points.
- Surprise a class with their beverage of choice and have it available at a break.
- Investing in a purified water dispenser is a great use of money, and many dispensers also provide hot water to make tea and other beverages. **I, S, S/E**

I = Intrinsic/Internal   E = Extrinsic/External   S/E = Social/Emotional
A = Attention   C = Control   S = Sensory   P = Pain   F = Fear   Esc = Escape

Get OUT of Here: Let children go outside after earning a break through good behavior. Give them a certain amount of time to just talk, socialize and hang out. These little breaks do take time, but work time is increased when behavior problems are reduced. Think about the amount of time saved in overall behavior management! **Esc, S/E, A**

Halvsies (Work Reduction Program): Establish steps for how kids can end up doing less work on a certain task or set of tasks! For instance, if a kid has exhibited a certain amount of good behavior, he only has to do half of an assignment. This is a really fun way to engage kids but will actually increase their productivity because although they are doing less, they may be more engaged in their work. **I, Esc, C**

I = Intrinsic/Internal   **E** = Extrinsic/External   **S/E** = Social/Emotional
A = Attention   **C** = Control   **S** = Sensory   **P** = Pain   **F** = Fear   **Esc** = Escape

NO MORE HOMEWORK: The benefits of homework can be debated anyway. Use no homework as a reinforcement: When students exhibit a particular behavior, they are excused from a homework assignment. Or, you can require students to reach a certain level or number of good behaviors to earn no homework. For instance, "If you are compliant and follow directions the first time during this lesson, you will have no homework." See how much behavior improves by not having homework for that day. **I, Esc, C**

Chatter Box: Choose some topics pertinent to the age group with which you are working. Have the child select which topic he wants to cover and then engage him in a conversation about that topic for a set amount of time. This also works in a group treatment setting. The important thing here is to get the children talking about anything. Communicating is a social skill that is learned like anything else, and so practice is important. Plus, it builds connections to the adult(s) in charge beyond the topic/lesson of that moment. **Esc, S/E, A**

I = Intrinsic/Internal   E = Extrinsic/External   S/E = Social/Emotional
A = Attention   C = Control   S = Sensory   P = Pain   F = Fear   Esc = Escape

Guaranteed Success: "Everyone has an A on this quiz—all you have to do is look at it!" Or, "All of you have 100% on this test: Now, do the best you can answering all the questions." Or, "Everyone write your name, favorite food and hobby on a sheet of paper, and you will have an A." This sets the stage for success and takes away the fear of failing. **I, F**

Presentation Picks: Anything that reduces anxiety is reinforcing. For example, a student is anxious about speaking to the group: Allow her to choose her output source: Poster board display, presentation, report, video, etc. **F, C**

I = Intrinsic/Internal   **E** = Extrinsic/External   **S/E** = Social/Emotional
A = Attention   **C** = Control   **S** = Sensory   **P** = Pain   **F** = Fear   **Esc** = Escape

◾ CHAPTER 8
Teaching New Skills

Discovering the function of a behavior and then, the motivation of the individual exhibiting the behavior is the key to changing behavior. Remember, a functional behavioral assessment looks beyond the overt behavior and examines significant, child-specific, social, sensory, physical, affective, cognitive and/or environmental factors associated with the occurrence and non-occurrence of specific behaviors. This broader perspective gives you a better understanding of the purpose (function) behind the child's behavior. Interventions based on understanding "why" a person misbehaves are extremely useful in addressing a wide range of behavior issues.

We've given you many ideas for how to set up reinforcement plans that are based on the motivation of the child exhibiting the inappropriate behavior. At the same time, we need to teach each student a better, more acceptable way of getting his needs met (based on the function of the behavior). The replacement skill must be a reciprocal match for the function of the inappropriate behavior. For a behavior plan to be truly successful, it must include not only a way to reduce inappropriate behaviors but also a plan to teach the student appropriate replacement skills. A general approach to take when considering teaching replacement skills is

- Identify behaviors that need replacing and their function.
- Identify appropriate alternative behaviors that meet the same function.
- Teach/reteach replacement behaviors and attach a powerful payoff (reinforcers).
- Provide reminders (visual, verbal) about using replacement behaviors.
- Have the peer group also reinforce the replacement behaviors.

Some common replacement skills adults would want to teach to individual children to replace the inappropriate/ineffective behaviors are

- How to follow the plan (Plan A).
- How to go to Plan B when necessary.
- Learning to wait.
- Using coping skills.
- Using verbal, non-verbal and visual ways to communicate.
- Taking care of yourself.
- Problem solving.

HOW TO FOLLOW THE PLAN (PLAN A)

Whether the plan for a particular child is formal or informal, it is important to teach her how exactly she is supposed to follow the plan. Plan A is the original plan the child is supposed to be following. Some steps to remember:

1. Teach and reteach the routines of the plan. It really helps to make the plan visual so there is clarity and less confusion. With older kids (high school) verbal reminders are often enough, but kids who have difficulty with verbal instruction might need written or visual reminders.
2. Next, teach/show/demonstrate the benefit of following the plan.
3. Show the child how to access the plan (e.g., look at a visual, ask someone).

HOW TO GO TO PLAN B

Plan B is the go-to plan when Plan A (your original plan) is not working or for some reason there is interference with plan progression. Having a Plan B is very helpful in crisis situations and with people who tend to get angry when overwhelmed. Some steps to remember:

1. Identify the current response to behavior-inducing situations.
2. Identify what the appropriate Plan B would be (alternative/replacement behavior).
3. Use a multifaceted approach in teaching Plan B that might include
   a. Visually depicting the situation/response.
   b. Verbally rehearsing/role-playing the situation/response.
   c. Pictorially depicting the situation/response (e.g., social stories, cards, charts).
   d. Having the kid view other students exhibiting appropriate responses (i.e., learning from others).
   e. Giving verbal/visual reminders before entering situations.
   f. Utilizing powerful reinforcement for using Plan B.

LEARNING TO WAIT

Following are some ways to teach the skill of waiting appropriately:

- Identify the situation in which waiting is required.
- Provide a visual cue that indicates to the student to wait. This could be a small piece of construction paper that says "Wait" on it or a picture of someone waiting.
- The wait card could also have pictures/words that tell the student what he can do while he waits (e.g., spell his name, play with squishy ball, count to 10).
- When introducing the concept of the wait card, hold a desired item for the student. Hand her the wait card and wait for 1 or 2 seconds before praising her and giving her the desired item. Gradually increase the time the student waits before receiving the desired item.
- Use in the natural environment.

USING COPING SKILLS

Coping skills can include a variety of replacement behaviors, such as relaxation skills, impulse control skills, seeking appropriate sensory input and use of social skills. These skills can be taught one on one or in a social skills group. It's very important that the students have opportunities to practice the skills when they are calm. To expect a student to easily use a coping skill when he is upset is unreasonable. It will take practice, prompts and shaping procedures to teach a student to generalize a coping skill. A general procedure for teaching coping skills are:

- Talking about situations in which a coping skill/social skill is needed.
- Modeling the skill.
- Practicing many times with the student(s) the specific coping or social skill.
- Reinforcing the student for exhibiting skill while practicing.
- Making sure the student uses the coping skill in the natural environment and reinforcing at a higher level when this occurs.

USING LANGUAGE OR VISUAL ASSISTS TO COMMUNICATE

We've discussed previously that in general, behavior is communication. For many kids, it is easier to exhibit an inappropriate behavior to communicate their needs than it is to use their language skills in an appropriate manner. We need to teach these kids that there are acceptable ways to communicate their feelings. Some verbal, nonverbal and visual strategies that can be taught as replacement skills are

- Showing a break card to an adult when the child needs to leave a situation or be allowed to step back from a task.
- Using "Rage Cycle," "3/5 Point Scale" or "Zones of Regulation" programs for a child to communicate how she is feeling and what she needs to do at specific times.
- Practicing using verbal and nonverbal communication skills in a variety of situations.
- Using assistive technology devices (high tech and low tech) to communicate wants, needs and feelings.

TAKING CARE OF YOURSELF

Teaching kids the basic skills to take care of themselves is important and will often head off or help to minimize behaviors:

- Stay hydrated.
- Get enough sleep/practice good sleep hygiene.
- Eat well/have healthy snacks.
- Take your medication if needed/as prescribed.
- Have physical outlets/get exercise.
- Essentially, consider your basic needs.

PROBLEM SOLVING

1. Teach a person a problem-solving method that works for him. For instance, sometimes it helps to have it in written format. Other times, it is helpful to talk out the problem. Some overall approaches you can use to help someone solve problems are as follows:
   a. Is it hard/difficult or easy/simple? Can I help?
   b. Is this a big deal or a little deal? Let's look at this together.
   c. Are you ready/not ready? How can I help get you ready?
   d. Is this scary or not scary? Let's look at how to make it less scary.
   e. Can you do anything about it? If yes, then you have control.
      If not, then this is beyond your control.
   f. Is this something you like to do or not?

2. Another easy way to break down problem solving is to use the P.A.S.S. approach developed for use with kids with Oppositional Defiant Behavior:
   P = Problem: What is the problem exactly?
   A = Assess: Assess the situation. Look at safety first and then whether the problem is within your ability to solve or whether you need help.
   S = Strategies: Identify strategies to get you through the problem.
   S = Solution: Pick a strategy and implement. Continuing to think about it will not get you out of the problem. This is the action step.

Section IV

LEVEL 3:
NEGATIVE BEHAVIORS

Not able to be successful in given environment	Possibility of getting hurt or hurting others	Actually hurting self or others	Damaging property

Running away	Severe medical or psychiatric symptoms	Legal violations

CHAPTER 9

Reaction Plans for Calming Students

Behaviors preventing learning and/or success in a given environment and those causing injury or destruction are obviously the most serious. These are the behaviors that we categorize as Level 3. Adults working with students on Level 2 are using an individual reinforcement plan as well as teaching replacement behaviors. Often students continue to display disruptive behaviors at times, even when Level 2 strategies are being used. These disruptive behaviors need to be addressed by adults using Level 3 interventions.

Level 3 interventions include plans that help students and adults with strategies to calm and regroup, ideas for environmental reaction plans and instructions for working with students when a safe room is utilized. These Level 3 strategies will work hand in hand with Level 2 strategies. Staff should always be referring back to the Level 2 strategies because they are the basis for good programming. The Level 3 strategies help staff and students react when behaviors escalate, but the Level 2 strategies should always be in place. Refer to Chapters 7, 8 and 9 for more information on Level 2 strategies.

During a crisis, many things can happen including: Physical aggression to others or property, self-harm, verbal threats, verbal aggression without threats, rage and panic. Having a system in place that can help you address all of these issues will be very helpful.

Think of this example to help understand the importance of having a system in place: Many of us take C.P.R./First aid classes so that in the event of an emergency we are prepared for what to do as the medical event happens and even after the immediate assessment, triage and treatment has occurred. Having this training helps us deal with a medical crisis should it arise. This gives us some ability to help another person while having a plan in place to render that help. More important though is that it gives the recipient a much better chance at survival in the event they need the help.

Think of learning about behavior escalation and crisis as the same as C.P.R. and First Aid training only now we are looking at behavioral emergencies. Fortunately, these emergencies are often not life threatening ending up in a call to 911!"

CRISIS CYCLE AND RESPONSES

People go through crisis situations either individually or with another person in the midst of a conflict of some sort. Depending on a variety of factors, the crisis can become severe, involving the safety of self and others. Even when a crisis is less severe, it can still be impactful for that person and relationships she has with others. Following is a diagram of a crisis cycle.

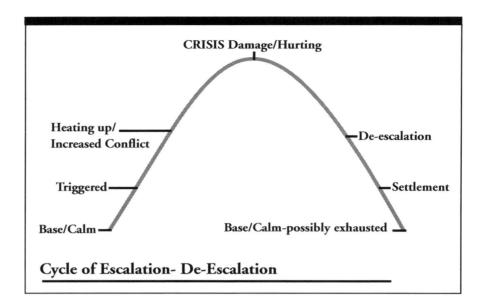

Cycle of Escalation- De-Escalation

The cycle starts with Base/Calm and moves through various stages, then back toward Base/Calm-possibly exhausted. However, not everyone moves through each stage. Hopefully, a crisis can be headed off completely, and this keeps everyone involved safer and lessons the overall impact of the crisis.

There are several factors that can make a crisis or conflict more likely:

- Exhaustion
- Being hungry/dehydrated
- Mental health issues
- Medical issues
- Cognitive abilities
- Sensory issues

The Base/Calm stage is easy. During this stage, keep doing what you have been doing! Basically, follow the reinforcement/motivation plan that has been set up. In this stage, everything is going fine, and of course you want to maintain that as much as possible.

Triggered Stage: If possible, try to eliminate or at least mitigate triggers that were previously identified. Think of a trigger as the spark for the fire. Eliminate the spark, and the fire never gets going.

Heating Up/Increased Conflict: During this phase, an individual is starting to become angry, or two or more people are engaging in conflict with each other. For the individual, it will be important to provide him with appropriate options within safe limits. For people engaging in conflict with each other, it is usually best to let them solve their conflicts, as long as they can remain safe with each other. Rushing in and trying to solve an escalated conflict often does not work, and then the intensity increases. You should get involved if there is a significant power differential between the two parties and/or the conflict is becoming unsafe and/or abusive.

CRISIS/Damage/Hurting: At this stage, the person is in a total crisis, and emotional or even physical damage may be occurring. People engaged in this phase will be hurting each other emotionally and possibly physically. The response is rather simple but difficult to do unless you are safe and calm: Interact only when necessary to maintain safety for all involved.

De-escalation: Cooling off procedures are the most effective during this phase. For instance, physical activities (e.g., deep breathing) might be helpful. It is important to remember that de-escalation happens after a crisis, but a person can go into another crisis quickly unless she is taught and sometimes assisted with appropriate ways to cool down.

Settlement: In this stage, the individual or group involved in the conflict has reached a point at which they are not in crisis and are able to be rational. They are calm and can process information. The conflict is over and has been resolved, at least for the time being.

Base/Calm-possibly exhausted: The person has returned to his usual level of functioning. However, if he was in a serious crisis, he might be exhausted and physically and mentally still at risk. (This is especially true during restraint and physical altercations.) It will be necessary to provide support and appropriate observation at this stage to maintain safety.

Again, it is important to remember that not everyone goes through a crisis in the same manner; some people hover in the trigger or heating up phase but do not go into a full crisis. Below is a quick guide for responses under each category:

- **Base/Calm:** Continue current plan, approach and programming. Adjust as needed.
- **Trigger:** Remove the trigger if possible, remove person from the trigger and utilize replacement skill behaviors.
- **Heating Up/Increased Conflict:** Offer appropriate choices within limits. Do not engage in power struggles. Allow people to safely solve their own conflicts.
- **Crisis/Damage:** The first thing is to keep everyone safe. Interact only when necessary. Give space and time. Utilize approved safety procedures.
- **De-escalation:** Use appropriate cooling off strategies, avoiding re-escalation. Do not discuss the issue(s) at this time.
- **Settlement:** Use problem solving. Assist in returning to routines, schedules, etc.
- **Base/Calm:** Use observation and support, with medical follow up if needed. Return to usual activities. Do not return to the trigger activity.

Even if you cannot follow all of these steps, you can follow an easy-to-remember system called the "3-D's of Rage." This is an easy plan to help with the top part of the cycle of escalation. Dealing with rage in the moment is helpful for nearly every area of oppositional defiant behavior.

3-D'S OF RAGE

Using easy-to-remember steps is best, as it is difficult to remember things when under stress:

1. **Diffuse:** Utilize immediate steps to break the rage up into smaller, manageable bits to make things easier to deal with.

    Examples of Diffusion: Break up the task, utilize more frequent breaks, use a mini-schedule, offer some options that can help in the moment, remain calm.

2. **Distract:** Move attention towards something, somewhere or someone else

   Examples of Distract: Leave the area or remove triggers, use visuals, engage in jobs or diversionary activities away from conflict and/or trigger.

3. **De-escalate:** Help a person move down the cycle of crisis and to a better place physically and emotionally. Examples: Physical activities (e.g., walking, running, exercises), sense-based activities, mental/emotional activities (e.g., talking, counting, breathing, processing, resting).

Whereas it is necessary to consider your individual situation when using these steps, remembering the 3-D's can be a great framework from which to operate. Having a system for what you do, especially in a time of crisis, is the most efficient and certainly the easiest way to function.

Finally, having the escalation plan reaction steps posted in a nearby area or by the safe room is another good way to help remember steps to take. We rely on visuals on a daily basis to help us remember what to do even in non-crisis situations. In a crisis, having visual and even auditory remainders can make a major difference.

TYPES OF REACTION PLANS

When you are working with a student who can display Level 3 behaviors, using a reaction plan is a great strategy. They serve as visual way to help students and adults know what to do at each phase of the behavior cycle. We know that when upset (child or adult), a person is not able to access previously learned information easily. Therefore, a visual reaction plan reminds the student and the adult how to act at each stage of the behavior cycle. One example of a visual reaction plans is the 3-Point Scale.

3-Point Scale

We developed our own 3-point scale, based on "The Incredible 5-Point Scale" by Kari Dunn Buron (http://www.5pointscale.com). Our 3-Point Scale is a visual tool to help adults and kids identify behaviors on three levels:

1. When I'm Feeling Good/Doing What I Should (#1 on the chart)
2. When I'm Starting to Get Upset (#2 on the chart)
3. When I'm Really Upset (#3 on the chart)

The 3-Point Scale template includes a column that describes what the behavior looks like/feels like, a column that tells the kid what she should do at that level and a column that tells the adult how he should react when the kid is at each level. The adult should fill out the chart with the kid. You can even add visuals or color code each level to help the kid better utilize the strategies. The goal is to help the kid keep her behaviors at Level 1 or to bring her behavior down from Level 2 to Level 1 or from Level 3 to Level 2 and finally to Level 1.

Reaction Plan
3-Point Scale - Child Sample

Rating	Looks Like and Feels Like	Adult Will:	I Will:
3	**Rage/Upset** spitting, screaming, using hurtful words, running Go to the Quiet Room	• Help support you • Help guide you to the Quiet Room • Close the door • Not talk until you are ready	• Be quiet • Close my eyes
2	**Start to Get Upset/ Frustrated** stressed out, walking around out of seat, need a break to calm down Go to room 300 for a 5-minute break	• Help support you • Allow you to play with a ball, draw a picture, play with legos or play mousetrap	• Play with a ball • Draw a picture • Play with legos • Play mousetrap
1	**Great or Good!** • I feel comfortable to be in class • I can stay in class and participate with my friends.	• Help support you • Help answer your questions	• Sit in my chair • Listen to the person talking • Raise my hand if I have a question • Do my work in class • Talk quietly with friends when it's ok to talk • I can take a 5-minute break in room 300 if I complete five tasks

Reaction Plan
3-Point Scale

Rating	Looks Like and Feels Like	Adult Will:	I Will:
3			
2			
1			

Adult Reaction Plan-Adult Sample

Rating	Looks Like and Feels Like	Adult Will:
3	• Aggressive toward adults/peers • Climbs under table • Throws items • Yelling	• Evacuate the area and let him go under cubby/table to calm down • Call K (C if K is gone) • Use deflection/positioning to avoid aggression and use approved restraint if necessary for safety • Ignore negative comments toward adults/crying for Mom • If he makes negative comments about self, staff will make short statements affirming his goodness • When he is calm, sit him in a chair and problem-solve with Cartoon Conversations • Return him to classroom after completing a short task to demonstrate compliance • Communicate to parent/fill out documentation
2	• Head goes down • Says "I'm bored" • Plays with shoes, lies on floor during rug time	• Give alternative work to try and keep positive momentum going • If that doesn't break the cycle, tell student he is going to take a break and call to the Resource Room/Office for staff to get him • Resource/Office staff work with student, and he participates in activities/completes work (first/then) and then returns to his classroom
1	• Follows directions • Sits quietly • Does assigned work • Appropriate interactions with peers	• Color in items on behavior chart • Give verbal praise • Leave dogs on his chart for no blurting out • Give special privileges (e.g., jobs, errands, stickers)

Rumble, Rage and Recovery Plan

The concept of looking at three areas of behavior cycles, rumble, rage and recovery (especially for students on the Autism spectrum), was developed by Brenda Smith Myles in her book *Asperger Syndrome and Difficult Moments*. We have designed a template that tells adults what strategies to use with individual students based on what stage they are in. Myles believes that when students become aggressive, they go through each stage (rumble, rage and recovery), and we need to help them through each one. Our interventions should be stronger in the rumble stage to try and calm the student down. The ideas for rage and recovery tell us what to do to help the student be safe as she progresses through those stages. Following are a blank template for a Rumble, Rage and Recovery Plan and an example filled out for a student. In the example, the italicized print shows what behaviors the student demonstrates at each stage; underneath is what the adult should do.

Reaction Plan
Rumble, Rage and Recovery - Sample

Rumble Stage	Rage Stage	Recovery Stage
Revving Up **Agitated/Distressed**	**Out of Control** **Unsafe**	**Calming Down** **Cooling Off**
Picks fingers *Rocks back and forth* *Repeats words*	*Crawls under table and throws things* *Head bangs on floor*	*Sits in bean bag chair*
Fiddle Items	Remove other kids to safety	Does pop beads
Sensory Room break	Remove items to be thrown	Bring a small cup of water to him
Listen to music	No talking: Refer to visual picture on calming down	Once done with pop beads, have him check schedule

Reaction Plan
Rumble, Rage and Recovery

Rumble Stage	Rage Stage	Recovery Stage
Revving Up	Out of Control	Calming Down
Agitated/Distressed	Unsafe	Cooling Off

ZONES OF REGULATION

This tool provides a visual way to help kids know how they are feeling. Adults teach students how to move through the zones to get/stay at the green zone. The curriculum comes with pictures to help kids recognize how they are feeling. According to the "The Zones of Regulation®" website (2011, Social Thinking Publishing), the tool is a curriculum comprising lessons and activities designed by Leah Kuypers, M.A.Ed., OTR/L. The Zones is a systematic, cognitive behavioral approach used to teach self-regulation by categorizing all the different ways we feel and states of alertness we experience into four concrete zones. The Zones curriculum provides strategies to teach students to become more aware of and independent in controlling their emotions and impulses, managing their sensory needs and improving their ability to problem solve conflicts.

Blue Zone

Stretch

Green Zone

Drink Water

Yellow Zone

Deep Breaths

Red Zone

Take a Break

Safety Plan

A safety plan is an intervention developed by the team working with the student who is displaying Level 3 behaviors. The Safety Plan lists the behaviors of concern and states what kinds of strategies have worked in calming the student down when upset and what strategies do not work in calming the student down. The plan then details what steps adults should take in helping the student, his peers and adults be safe. The plan also indicates who should do what task to make sure all steps are covered correctly. The Safety Plan also requires signatures from each team member (including parents) to indicate their agreement with the procedure. Following is a blank Safety Plan template and an example of one that has been filled out.

Safety Plan
Individual Student - Sample

Name: _Elementary Ethan_

Date plan was initiated: _____ Review Dates: _____

Medical/Psychiatric/Mental Health Information:

Medical Alert: _____

Other Information: _Does better with male staff when upset_

Description of Specific Unsafe Behaviors:

Hits staff with a closed fist in the chest and stomach area. Ethan kicks staff 3–4 times in succession in their lower leg area, usually causing bruising.

Warning Signs/Triggers	Strategies That Work	Strategies That Don't Work
• High noise • Enjoyable activity is stopped • Verbal threats/moves toward staff	• Calm voice • Move away • Acknowledge his emotions • Give Choices	• Don't force compliance • Don't state negative consequences • Don't raise your voice

Crisis Response Plan

What to do if the student exhibits above described behavior:	Who will do what/back up staff?
1. Move away and give verbal reassurance and visual cue card. 2. If behavior continues, for more than 1 minute, remove class and call for Mr. Smith. 2 People must be present. 3. If staff cannot move away from him, then staff may use a Mandt restraint for the shortest time need 4. As Ethan calms down and stabilizes, allow him time to draw. 5. Mr. Smith will document on Critical Incident Report 6. Mr. Smith/Administrator will call parent.	Mr. Smith Administrators (all are Mandt trained)

Student Safety Team Members: (Include IEP Team, Paraeducators, Administrator, Nurse, Parent/Guardian)

Name/Signature	Title	Date
_____	_____	_____
_____	_____	_____
_____	_____	_____
_____	_____	_____

Safety Plan
Individual Student

Name: _____

Date Plan Was Initiated: _____ Review Dates: _____

Medical/Psychiatric/Mental Health Information:

Medical Alert: _____

Other Information: _____

Description of Specific Unsafe Behaviors:

Warning Signs/Triggers	Strategies That Work	Strategies That Don't Work

Crisis Response Plan

What to do if the student exhibits above described behavior:	Who will do what/back up staff?

Student Safety Team Members: (Include IEP Team, Paraeducators, Administrator, Nurse, Parent/Guardian)

Name/Signature	Title	Date

■ CHAPTER 10

Environmental Reaction Plans and Staff Training

VOLUNTARILY LEAVING AN AREA

We always want to use the least restrictive way of interacting with an escalated student to avoid physically intervening. These strategies are more effective if used before the student gets to too high a level in the crisis cycle. Some strategies for adults to use to prompt the student to leave an area voluntarily are as follows:

- **Use of break card.** The student can initiate the use of the break card to leave a classroom/area. Putting the card on the teacher's desk, leaving it on the student's desk, holding it up in the air as she gets up to leave or putting it in an envelope by the door on his/her way out are examples of how the student can use the break card. Adults and students need to know where the student will take her break and what the student will do during that time (e.g., put head down, walk two laps around the gym, look at a book), so preplanning needs to occur. The goal here is to avoid further escalation in a large group to keep everyone safe.

- **Adult cues.** The adult can also initiate the use of the break card by unobtrusively placing it on the student's desk or quietly saying "Break time" as you near the student. The teacher can also use a hand cue (pointing to the door, for example) or a number cue (e.g., "3" relates to where the student is on his 3-point scale) to prompt the student to leave the room.

- **Out-of-the-classroom conversation.** Students don't like to be called out in front of their peers. If the student is escalating, the adult can ask the student to have a conversation in the hallway. The adult, especially one with a positive relationship with the student, might be able to calm the student down enough to re-enter the classroom successfully, or if the student's behavior is still escalating, the adult can direct the student to where she needs to go or ask for help. One benefit of this technique is that the student is out of the classroom already if she continues to escalate.

- **Use of the schedule.** The teacher can be flexible and change up the student's schedule so that the task is quickly finished and it's break time next. Once again, the goal is not to "give in" to the student but to keep the student from escalating in a large group.

- **Antiseptic bouncing.** This term refers to sending the student on an errand to break the escalation cycle. Have some premade notes ready for the student to take to the office or another teacher, give him a book to return to the library or have him find the custodian to get some supplies.

ESCORTING FROM AN AREA

Systems should be in place ahead of time in the event that a child will need to be escorted from an area. Specifically, adults need to know the following:

1. When will we escort a child to another setting?
2. How will we decide when that action is needed?
3. Are staff able to do an escort safely?
4. Where will we take the child?
5. What is the return plan or plan after the escort has happened?

Certainly, it is always necessary to know your physical limits and also the regulatory and legal limits within your particular area. Of particular note is to realize that escorting someone to another environment during a time of crisis can often lead to a situation in which restraint may be needed.

CLEARING THE AREA WITH AN EVACUATION PLAN

Sometimes, a better option than physically escorting someone into another environment is to have a system in place that allows for a safe evacuation plan of others in the area. Again, having a plan is vital. For example, it is common and often mandatory practice to have children practice fire drills. This is a system that is in place that works very well, ensuring that in the event of an actual fire, everyone will know exactly what to do.

We suggest having a plan that utilizes an easy-to-use phrase or cue with children that indicates it is time to evacuate the room. The evacuation could be for any reason, such as behavior episodes, a child getting sick, a strange smell or an insect or animal infiltration. The reason for leaving is not important; rather, what is important is that the children understand that when they are cued, they need to exit safely and calmly.

To create the best chance of an evacuation working if needed, it will be necessary to practice (just like a fire drill) so that everyone is on the same page. Also, it is important to remember that evacuations change the environment; it may help the person in crisis to have fewer people around.

PLAN B

Plan B is simply having an alternative for when Plan A does not work. Having the skill to think about and pursue alternative options is very important when dealing with young people prone to behavioral issues. ALthough Plan B was covered in the Level 2 section, we discuss it again here because it is so important to use a Plan B when you end up working with a kid whose behaviors are in Level 3.

Plan B is the go-to plan when Plan A (your original plan) is not working or for some reason, there is interference with plan progression. Plan B is very helpful in crisis situations and with people who tend to get angry when overwhelmed.

- Identify the current response to behavior-inducing situations.
- Identify what the appropriate Plan B would be (alternative/replacement behavior).
- Use a multifaceted approach in teaching Plan B, which might include

- Visually depicting the situation/response.
- Verbally rehearsing/role-playing the situation/response.
- Pictorially depicting the situation/response (e.g., social stories, cards, charts).
- Having the child view other students exhibiting appropriate responses (learning from others).
- Giving verbal/visual reminders before entering situations.
- Utilizing powerful reinforcement for using Plan B.

POSSIBLE STAFF TRAINING AGENDAS AND TOPICS

This section is intended to give you a guide for possible discussion and training topics for your staff when dealing with kids with problematic behaviors.

Administrators and supervisors will find this section particularly helpful, especially for those who are in charge of trainings, meetings and overall management of behavior. Consider your environment and work setting and use this outline as a platform from which to spring when thinking about ideas for managing behavior.

Each section has an issues/concerns statement that you can adjust to your situation. Following is a topic of discussion and a mini-outline of items on which you might want to touch. These are some things to keep in mind:

1. Keep kids safe: At a minimum, do no harm.
2. Relationships are paramount for growth.
3. Communication is the key.
4. Maintain emotional and physical safety for adults and children at the same time.
5. Keep doing what works and change what is not working.
6. Work as a team.

Issues/Concerns

Behaviors from certain kids are emerging or demanding all of staff time, and/or it is transition time or a new part/the beginning of a term.

Building Healthy Relationships

- Spend time discussing students
  - Identify relationships that students have already.
  - Begin work on establishing new relationships.
  - Discuss whether there are any students that have been missed.
- Team approach
  - Build teams around challenging students.
  - Teams create safety for children as well as adults.
  - Teams also allow for one adult to relieve another during crisis moments.
  - Teams create better opportunities for accurate documentation.

Issues/Concerns

Interactions between adults and children/youth are becoming negative or quickly turn into verbal or even physical altercations.

Building Healthy Communication

- Nonverbal elements of communication
  - What is our physical presence saying to students?
  - Are we smiling at students? Do our facial expressions match what we are saying?
- Verbal elements of communication
  - Are we using words that our students understand?
  - Are we using student names when speaking with them?
- Behavior as communication
  - What does our behavior tell students?
  - Do we look at student behavior as a form a communication?
  - What is _____ [student behavior] telling us?
- Alternative communication
  - Do we have students who communication primarily nonverbally?
  - Do we need to look at ways to improve our listening skills with students with communication impairments?
- Crisis situations: Have we identified triggers as to how this person escalates, and are we looking at how our behaviors play into the crisis?

Issues/Concern

Communication and conflict difficulties are occurring, especially during crisis situations. Communication and conflict styles need to be matched with the needs of children/youth in your particular environment.

Building Healthy Conflict Resolution

- Communication styles
  - What is your style of communication?
  - How does your style work or not work with students?
- Confrontation during conflict: I messages and you messages (practice).
- Empathy in communication: How do you show empathy?
- Conflict outcomes: Win/win, win/lose, lose/lose. Are we striving for win/win as much as possible?
- Crisis situations
  - Identifying staff responses.
  - Practicing staff responses.
  - Plugging a specific student into a crisis cycle and developing appropriate responses.
  - Developing a plan to mitigate triggers and avoid escalations.

Issues/Concerns

Kids are displaying physical aggression, and you have restraint-associated concerns.

Proper Restraint Methods, Risk and Medical Issues

1. Do we have students we are restraining?
2. Do we need to receive restraint training from a certified organization?
3. Do we understand the risks of restraint use (physical, psychological/emotional, and legal)?
4. What are the factors that increase and decrease injury risk?
5. What are the restraint responses that indicate distress?
6. What are the positional risks (standing, sitting, prone/supine) that are not allowed or recommended?
7. What are the considerations for the restraint of small children?
8. What are the emergency responses (safety plans/medical emergencies)?
9. Consider modifying or practicing the area specific to your students.

Technical Skills

Staff should be trained in an official program for how to safely restrain others. The recommendation is to use an approved restraint system.

- Staff may need a review on technical skills.
- Prohibited practices: Review practices that are prohibited in your situation.
- Consider the following information in terms of individual students and review accordingly:
  - Body positioning and movement
  - Escorting
  - Stimulus transfer/transfer of aggression
  - Restraint situations/techniques
  - One person
  - More than one person
  - Going to the floor (not a takedown)
  - Shorter people/smaller stature
  - Special applications
  - Separation skills
    - Wrists
    - Fingers
    - Clothing
    - Biting
    - Hair pulling
    - Separating people

ADMINISTRATOR PRACTICE

Following are two lists that we feel will be helpful for administrators and supervisors. It is essential for administrators to remember that staff are looking to you for guidance and security.

We always need direction from our leaders, especially in times of trouble. In working with children and youth with behavioral issues, a poor administrative team can quickly escalate behaviors and also leave staff feeling unsupported, frustrated and even injured.

Administrator Practices to Which to Adhere

1. Support your staff emotionally and sometimes physically.
2. Ask for input regarding disciplinary measures.
3. Empathize with staff.
4. Respond as quickly as possible during a crisis.
5. Stay current on best practices.
6. Build strong relationships with staff, parents and children.
7. Participate in Level 1 and Level 2 interventions/programming.
8. Demonstrate mutual respect and provide appropriate team-building opportunities.
9. Reinforce your staff with what they find motivating: Remember, motivational schemes are for adults too!

Administrator Practices to Consider and/or Question

1. Do not ask your staff to do things that you would not do. If you haven't done it yourself, then do not ask someone else to do it.
2. Do not undermine staff plans and procedures.
3. Avoid using outdated interventions and techniques.
4. Avoid escalating during a crisis. If you cannot handle the situation, ask for assistance. Escalating will not help anyone. Staff need to feel you can handle matters.
5. Do not get trapped in thinking "It's not fair to the rest of the kids." That type of thinking is based in fear, not fact.
6. Avoid blaming others; work with them, not over them.
7. Be willing to accept help from outside resources.
8. Be willing to accept the fact that people working for you often have special expertise and sometimes know much more than you. That is not a threat to your position; it is a reality. Use it to help the child/child's team progress and move forward.

◼ CHAPTER 11
Safe Rooms

We consider the use of safe rooms to be an appropriate and improved alternative over restraint/physical interventions. Typically, a safe room environment is used to keep a child safe, keep others safe or provide an educational/therapeutic program that is appropriate for a child's needs.

Safe rooms are also called time-out rooms, quiet places and seclusion areas. Safe rooms should be designed to keep both kids and adults safe and of course should maintain an atmosphere of dignity and respect.

There should be a system in place that indicates the steps for how a child might end up in the safe room and how he will leave that situation. Usually, a crisis of some sort leads the way into the safe room. As stated earlier, it is necessary to have appropriate preplanned steps and a visual system to provide everyone with structure for what to do during a crisis. Following is an example of a system you might want to utilize when thinking about using a safe room:

1. Crisis Situation: Child is in the midst of a crisis and needs additional intervention.
2. Safe room is accessed, and child is in the safe room. Adults need to decide if the door should be closed or open.
3. Any dangerous items should be removed from the safe room. Depending on the situation, this might include clothing, such as belts, shoelaces or other items, that could compromise safety.
4. Child might need access to comfort items and/or sensory items that are appropriate.
5. Adults should follow all posted procedures.
6. An exit strategy should be in place at the moment the safe room is used.

In some programs, the safe room is used as an alternative area for learning or therapeutic intervention. This type of environment can be very effective. However, it is important to make sure that we clarify how the room is being used, as the intent in this example is different than when used during a crisis.

Safe rooms are an effective tool and create more safety for everyone involved. The use of restraint can also be minimized by the use of safe rooms. The following sections are guides and forms suggesting effective systems for implementing a safe room environment in your school or agency:

1. Safe Room Guidelines Checklist (overall use): Guides staff on proper development.

2. Safe Room Guide (posted by the safe room): System for using the room.

3. Safe Room Summary (data purposes)

4. Safe Room Tracking Sheet (data and documentation)

5. Safe Room Letter to Parent

6. Safe Room Crisis Response Guide (posted by the safe room); Used to help guide adults during a crisis within the safe room setting; might also want to think about posting the individual plan for the child and predetermined coping skills

Safe Room Guide
Checklist

☐ Use of safe room is endorsed by the school and/or agency and is incorporated as part of a continuum of behavioral interventions within agency policy.

☐ Safe room program has been risk assessed in relation to client/child and staff safety and is consistent with the agency occupational and safety guidelines/handbook and associated documents.

☐ Allows for meaningful educational and/or therapeutic activity to be provided for client/child.

☐ Has adequate ventilation, lighting and heat.

☐ Has adequate space for clients and staff.

☐ Allows arrangements for the client/child to have recess, lunch and toilet breaks when time occurs across those periods.

☐ Is conducive to de-escalating inappropriate behaviors.

☐ Is not to be locked, latched or secured in any way that would, in case of an emergency, prevent staff or the client/child from exiting the room.

☐ Is supervised at all times.

☐ Displays rules for behavior within the room.

☐ Displays school rules and expectations.

☐ Displays visual supports for de-escalation strategies and for appropriate behavior.

Communication and Evaluation

☐ Procedures for the use of the safe room have been communicated to all clients/children, parents/guardians and school staff.

☐ Training has been conducted for staff in procedures for the use of the dedicated safe room.

☐ A record of the use of the dedicated safe room with each individual client/child and for each occasion is maintained.

☐ Procedures for notifying parents or carers of the use of the time out room with their child have been developed.

☐ Procedures for referral or re-referral to an appropriate support team or client/child welfare team have been developed.

☐ A register of the use of the dedicated safe room is maintained and forwarded to the agency director.

☐ Procedures to be followed if a client/child does not comply with the use of the safe room or if the use of the use of the safe room is not successful in managing the behavior of the client/child have been developed.

☐ Data on the use of the safe room are used to assess its effectiveness in supporting an individual client/child.

☐ Data on the use of the safe room are used to assess the effectiveness of the strategy within the context of the regular review of the agency discipline policy.

Safe Room Guide
System for Using the Room

1. What time is it? Mark down the time that the child entered the room on the tracking sheet. Is the door closed? Mark down on the tracking sheet if and when the door was closed.

   _____

2. Call/radio additional support.

   _____

3. Is the child safe? Are other children safe? Are you safe? Is your support present? Document on the tracking sheet.

   _____

4. If child is not safe inside the safe room, initiate safe room safety procedures.

   _____

5. If other children are not safe, initiate class/area evacuation procedures.

   _____

6. If you are not safe, call for additional support and maintain safety of self and other children.

   _____

7. Limit your conversation with the child to only necessary information.

   _____

8. Is the child engaged with his/her de-escalation process? (Should be visual for the child; i.e., words and/or pictures.)

   _____

9. Before the child leaves the room, we need to have a plan as to where the child should go and with whom.

   _____

10. Once child de-escalates, open the door (document time door opened) and begin exiting strategy.

    _____

11. Are you okay? (Look for physical signs.)

    _____

12. Let's return to _____. (Avoid returning to the task that caused an escalation in the first place.)

    _____

13. Implement an exit from the safe room and move on to routine and next step in schedule. Document the time that child left the safe room.

    _____

Data Collection

School/Organization: _____ Date: _____ From: _____

Time Period: _____

Total Number of Individual Uses of the Safe Room (**For Seclusion Only**: Each Use Will Have a Summary Sheet):

_____

_____

_____

_____

_____

_____

Total Number of Students With Whom the Room Was Used: _____

Signature: _____ Date: _____

Safe Room Summary

School/Organization:_____ Date:_____ From:_____

Time Period: _____

Total Number of Individual Uses of the Safe Room (**For Seclusion Only**: Each Use Will Have a Summary Sheet): _____

_____

_____

Total Number of Students With Whom the Room Was Used: _____

Signature: _____ Date: _____

Safe Room Guide
Data Collection and Documentation

Is This Room Being Used For:

_____

_____

☐ **Seclusion** (Document on Appropriate Form)

☐ **Non-seclusion** (Child and Staff Are Safe)

Name_____Date: _____

Staff Name(s): _____

Time Entered Safe Room: _____

Time Exited Safe Room: _____

Door Open: _____ Door Closed: _____ Time Closed: _____

Time Re-Opened: _____

Parent Notified? _____ Method: _____

Room Was Used For:

_____ Quiet Learning Environment

_____ De-Escalation/Calming Down

_____ Child Entered Room on Own Accord (e.g., to Work, Rest)

_____ As Part of the Child's Schedule

_____ Sensory Break

_____ Other: _____

Staff Member Completing This Form: _____

Safe Room Guide
Letter to Parent

School/Agency Information _____ Date: _____

Parent/Guardian Information

_____

_____

Re:

_____

Dear Parent,

This letter is a follow up to the phone call you received about the use of our safe room today with your child. The safe room was used from: _____(time) to _____(time) on _____ (date) because: _____

_____

We have accessed the services of the (please check):

☐ Therapeutic Team

☐ Medical Team

☐ Other_____

We continue to develop and refine programming needs for your child to assist with behavior needs. Your participation in this process is very welcome.

Please sign the slip below and return it to the school directly or by fax (###-####) or email (##@###).

Yours sincerely,

_____

I would like to be involved in the further development and enhancement of programming for my son/daughter _____ (yes or no).

I would like to be involved by (please check):

☐ Attend a meeting at the school

☐ Discussion by telephone

☐ Sending some information in writing or by email

Signed (Parent/Guardian)_____ Date: _____

Please print name here:_____

Return to:

_____

Safe Room Guide
Crisis Response

Responses for the Following Incidents:

"Crisis Within the Crisis"

Safe Room Unsafe Behaviors

Self-Harm Behaviors

Hitting/Kicking of Staff

Bodily Fluid Issues

PROBLEM: Child Is Engaging in Unsafe Behaviors Within Safe Room

- Assess situation/self:
  - Is child unsafe in safe room?
  - Always call for back up if alone and notify administrator.
  - Does child have item causing safety risk (e.g., belt, clothing, and classroom item)?
  - Is child causing safety risk with his body (e.g., punching wall, throwing body down)?
- Intervening: If substantial safety risk exists, then:
  - Move response team into the room and remove item using appropriate and safe separation techniques.

OR

  - Move toward a physical intervention inside the room (blocking or restraint if necessary).
  - Once child analyzes physical intervention, back off and assess situation again.
- Follow protocols for leaving the safe room once calm.

PROBLEM: Child Is Engaging in Self-Harm Behaviors in Safe Room

- Assess situation/self:
  - How is the child harming self (e.g., pinching, picking, biting, scratching, gouging, head banging, hitting, throwing body around)?
  - Always call for back up if alone and notify administrator.
  - Stay calm.
- If a substantial safety risk exists, then enter the room and do the following:
  - If child is pinching/picking/scratching/gauging/hitting self
  - Put a barrier between area being injured and child's hand, such as your hand, a paper towel, a pillow.

- If child is biting self:
    1) Put a barrier between child's mouth and the body part she is biting.
    2) Don't use your hand as a barrier.
    3) Depending on child, offer an appropriate item on which to chew.
- If child is head banging:
    1) Put a barrier between child's head and object, such as your hand, your arm, a pillow.
- If child is body throwing:
    1) Use your body to block him from hitting something dangerous.
    2) Use direct physical contact only as needed.
- Talking should be kept to an absolute minimum during this crisis.

| PROBLEM: Hitting and Kicking of Staff in Safe Room |

- Assess situation/self:
    - Always call for back up if alone and notify administrator.
    - Back away: You are being hit because you are too close to the child.
    - Avoid talking unless necessary.
- If child continues to come at you, then:
    - Use deflection techniques.
    - Engage child in side body hug or approved/safe restraint.
    - Release hold as soon as child engages in analyzing the hold.
- With assistance, you should be able to back away far enough to not get hit.

| PROBLEM: Bodily Fluid Issues in the Safe Room |

1. Assess situation/self:
    a. Always call for help if alone and notify administrator.
    b. Stay calm.
2. Do not react to the behavior by saying, "Stop that" or "Don't."
3. Spitting: Leave or move away/turn away so you are not getting spat on directly.
4. Child urinates/defecates: Safe room no longer suitable, so:
    a. Child needs to be removed from room to clean it. Where you move her depends on level of escalation.
    b. Provide suitable/temporary cover (e.g., towel, blanket).
    c. Say to child, "Let's go get cleaned up and put on clean clothes." Then walk with child to designated area to clean up and change child's clothes.
    d. If child will not leave area or it is unsafe to have him move, then one staff member will need to physically block the messy area while another staff member/custodian cleans.
    e. If child is calm once changed, don't return to safe room but to stabilization phase (might include returning to schedule).

REACTION SCENARIOS

Running

When a child is running/runs off, the first determination to make is about safety:

1. Where is the child going (e.g., into a street, on the playground)?
2. How many people are present to assist?
3. What is plan?

Having a system in place for these types of situations is vital. The first decision is whether to chase the child (if possible). We answer this question the same way we do for determining the need for any physical involvement:

1. If I get involved, will something worse happen? If so, I should back off.
2. If I do not get involved, will something worse happen? If so, I should pursue.

The numbers game is at play here; the more adults you have, the less of a safety risk there is because you can pursue, surround and move in at the appropriate time. Radios/cellular phones can be very useful in these situations.

If you are alone and a child is running, remember to call for help; keep yourself safe first, and then maintain visual contact as much as possible. In general, if a child leaves your premises, the police will need to be called.

Note: The running behavior described here is different than youth who run away from home for several hours or days at a time. Running away from home is a much more serious behavior and is dealt with in a different manner. (Discussed in Scott Walls' seminar, Oppositional and Defiant Children and Youth.)

Aggression Toward Staff

We suggest that when working with kids with challenging behaviors, all staff should be trained in a reputable, certified and safe method of de-escalation, crisis management and physical intervention/restraint. Simply knowing what to do can provide confidence and safety, and this makes a big difference.

Regardless of the reason, some kids will become aggressive toward staff. It is okay to defend yourself; however, it is also important to not cause any harm. Some important things to remember about aggression:

- Remember the escalation/de-escalation steps.
- Tell the person that she can leave (or make some other Plan B choice) instead of being aggressive.
- Utilize your surroundings to help keep you safe; for instance, put a table between you and the person who is aggressive.
- Call for help. Simply the act of calling for help can get the person to stop.

- If he is close to you, keep your hands in a position in front you; it will look like you are going to clap your hands or something similar. This conveys a confident but nonaggressive stance and also allows you a better chance at blocking a strike that comes toward you. Never keep your hands behind your back or in your pockets when someone is being aggressive.

Use of Restraint

In our opinion, restraint should only be used for the safety of the child or others. Adults using restraint should be trained, especially if restraint use is required in a particular work setting. Restraint is a very serious issue, and there are many layers to the use of restraint. Refer back to the earlier section for administrators/supervisors in Chapter 12; some of that material is directly related to restraint issues and staff training.

■ CHAPTER 12

Problem Solving After a Behavioral Crisis

When children are in the midst of a behavioral crisis, it is NOT the time to attempt problem solving. Often, if adults try to problem solve shortly after a child is calm after going through the crisis cycle, the child will re-escalate. Problem solving may have to occur at a later time, even the next day for some children. The goal of problem solving is to review the behavior episode to help the child avoid escalation in the future. Problem solving can take the form of conversation, drawing what happened or even circling pictures on a premade diagram of the incident and what to do next time for children who are not able to use language effectively.

PROBLEM SOLVING THROUGH CONVERSATION

The most common method of problem solving is conversation. As stated earlier, during a crisis, it is important to talk less and interact only when necessary. However, after a crisis, it is important to discuss issues, problem solve and of course teach methods and strategies to solve problems. An easy method is to break down the problem, offer options to assess the problem, create potential solutions and then allow for a decision.

Even though we usually want an action-oriented decision made, many kids are not ready to make a decision; this is fine as long as they are not in danger. Sometimes, we can re-escalate a kid by forcing him to make a choice when in fact he clearly is not ready to. Also, many kids feel better just talking through problems even though a final, definitive decision has not been made.

A good way to break down a problem is to use a model that is systematic and easy to use that can be adjusted to a child's ability level. The P.A.S.S. approach (described in Chapter 9) was developed for use with youth diagnosed with Oppositional Defiant Disorder and is utilized in Walls' presentations throughout the United States. Following is a review of P.A.S.S.:

   P = Problem: Help the youth identify exactly what the problem is. Use language that makes sense. The problem might be written down, drawn out or discussed. When people are in crisis, everything becomes a problem, so it is helpful to break down what the problem truly is. If there are multiple problems, break them up and use this strategy with each individual problem.

   A = Assess: At this stage, we are going to assess the problem in terms of safety, potential for harm and whether the problem could potentially violate a rule or law. Also, the person gets to assess whether the problem fits or does not fit into what is important in her life.

> **S = Strategies**: We are going to help the child identify potential strategies for the problem that was identified. Strategies should be based on the child's level of understanding and ability to implement those strategies.
>
> **S = Solution**: Here, the person can pick a solution from the strategies identified or at least consider a solution if he is not ready to choose. When considering a solution, the person can evaluate the potential of different strategies. If he is ready to take action, he can then move toward actually making a decision.

The following is an example of using the P.A.S.S. method with a 13-year-old who is having issues with becoming physical with others when he is upset.

> **P** = Hitting or shoving other kids when I become angry.
>
> **A** = Is it going to harm me? Maybe. Does it harm others? Yes. Is it illegal? Yes. Is it against the rules? Yes. Is it the right thing for me to do? No. Is what my mother wants or taught me? No. Does it make me feel good? No.
>
> **S** = When I become so upset that I want to hurt others, I can go to my cool-down area, talk to Mrs. Jones because she really helps, do my exercises to get rid of my energy, pet the therapy dog, sit down in a quiet corner or throw balls in the gym.
>
> **S** = My first choice is going to be to do my exercises, and then I am going to pet the dog. If the dog is not there, I'm going to talk with Mrs. Jones, and if she is not there, I am going to sit down in a quiet corner, and everyone else is going to leave me alone.

The point of teaching this method is to increase cognitive problem solving skills. When someone is thinking, she is more rational, and if she is more rational, then she is in much better control.

PROBLEM SOLVING THROUGH DRAWING

"Cartoon Strip Conversations" by Carol Gray, creator of "Social Stories," can be an effective way to support the instruction of appropriate interactions to children with language and social deficits. There are a variety of strategies in using drawings to problem solve with kids, including the use of "thinking bubbles" and "talking bubbles."

We have adapted the concept and developed a template that is quick and easy for adults to use when attempting problem solving with students. It's a good idea to have plenty of blank copies with you to problem solve at a moment's notice. This will work well with some students, whereas other students will need to have a more structured opportunity to problem solve after a behavioral crisis. A blank problem solving template follows.

Problem Solving Through Drawing

First …	Then …	Then …

Then …	My teacher was …	Next time, I will …

PROBLEM SOLVING THROUGH A PREMADE TEMPLATE

For some situations, adults may want to use a premade template that shows in three columns what behaviors occurred, what the result was and what the child could do next time. The information can either be presented in word format or picture format. Staff would circle the appropriate words.

Behavior	Results	Next Time
Hit	Time out	Ask for help
Kick	Called home	Use my break card
Push	Missed recess	Tell the teacher
Use bad words	Office referral	Take a deep breath
Spit	Other:	Use my clam down chart
Bite		Other:
Other:		

◼ CHAPTER 13

Conclusions

This book should help you deal with just about all behavioral situations in multiple environments. While we designed this book to be used from start to finish, you may have pulled out different parts that were useful to you. We hope that the book gives you good information and increased skills to move forward.

Remember the importance of systems when designing your programs for groups of children and youth but also that systems are necessary for individuals. As you have seen, we have described a number of systemic interventions and strategies in the book, and these ideas can be used in so many different environments.

The reason most behavioral approaches and programs fail or have minimal impact over the long term is due to five primary reasons:

1. We don't take enough time or any time at all in learning about functions of behavior. Remember as we stated before, behavior has a job to do (gain or avoid something) and all behavior is communication. To change behavior, one must understand that we need to teach language to communicate and then provide, teach and reinforce a new behavior to gain or avoid something.

2. Not understanding motivation: So many programs and approaches are based on one concept of reinforcement (if there is reinforcement). We are all motivated to behave in certain ways based on our motivation. To change our behavior, we must be motivated to do so in order to effect change for the longer periods of time and even for permanent change. It is relatively easy to get someone to change behavior in the short term simply by telling them to stop or create a small change in what they are doing. Long-term change is the goal in terms of behavior management and for that reason, we must address motivation.

3. The interventions typically used often lapse more into discipline and punishment rather than reinforcement. This happens especially when behaviors have escalated and adults are feeling pressured or burned out. The interventions we are suggesting hold a commonality in them in that we can always increase reinforcement.

4. Behavior change can be a slow process for some individuals. People often underestimate the power of reinforcement when trying to change behavior. If they can't find an effective reinforcer quickly, they lose hope. Keep conducting reinforcement inventories and exploring possibilities. Once you find an effective reinforcer you will be amazed at how it really does allow you to change behavior.

5. Staff we've worked with often fail to see the importance of teaching replacement skills. If you don't teach an appropriate replacement behavior, you're only halfway done with your behavior change project. Giving an individual a better way of communicating, using social skills, handling their rage, etc. is such a great conclusion to completing your mission of behavior change.

If you don't see progress immediately, don't give up! Analyze your plan and keep plugging away until you see success. Trust us, you will see progress if you consistently utilize these systems correctly!

References

For your convenience, we have established a dedicated website to download all the worksheets, exercises and handouts. This gives you a choice to photocopy from the book or printing. The handouts will all be labeled with the corresponding titles and pages.

go.pesi.com/bms

Alberto, P. A., & Troutman, A. C. (2012). *Applied Behavior Analysis for Teachers*. Pearson Education.

Buron, K. D., & Curtis, M. (2004). *Incredible 5-Point Scale Assisting Students with Autism Spectrum Disorders in Understanding Social Interactions and Controlling Their Emotional Responses*. Lenexa, KS: Autism Asperger Publishing Company.

Donnellan, A. M., et al. (1988). *Progress Without Punishment: Effective Approaches for Learners with Behaviour Problems*. New York: Teachers College Press.

Fouse, B., & Wheeler, M. (1997). *A Treasure Chest of Behavioral Strategies for Individuals With Autism*.

Gray, C. (1994). *Comic Strip Conversations*. Arlington, TX: Future Horizons, Inc.

Hodgdon, L. A. (1999). *Solving Behavior Problems in Autism (Visual Strategies Series)*. Troy, MI: Quirk Roberts Publishing.

La Vigna, G. W., & Donnellan, A. M. (1985). *Alternatives to Punishment: Solving Behavior Problems with Non-Aversive Strategies*. New York: Irvington.

Myles, B. S., & Southwick, J. (2005). *Asperger Syndrome and Difficult Moments: Practical Solutions for Tantrums, Rage and Meltdowns*. Lenexa, KS: Autism Asperger Publishing Company.

New Mexico Public Education Department. (2010). *Addressing Student Behavior: A Guide for All Educators. Conducting a Functional Behavioral Assessment Developing a Behavioral Intervention Plan*. Santa Fe, NM.

Partington, J., & Sundberg, M. (2001). *QuickTips. Series One: Behavioral Teaching Strategies*. Pleasant Hill CA: Behavior Analysts Inc.

Sundberg, M. L., & Partington, J. W. (1998). *Teaching Language to Children with Autism and Other Developmental Disabilities*. Concord, CA: AVB Press.

About the Authors

 **Scott D. Walls, MA, LIPC, CCMHC** is currently a mental health counselor, consultant and speaker in private practice in Lincoln, NE and is the founder and Director of KICKS Counseling and the Lincoln Karate Clinic.

Scott has served as a behavior specialist and psychotherapist in the public schools and both the non-profit and profit sectors and has provided therapy and consultation services for hundreds of children, teens and families in the Lincoln area. In addition, Scott has provided professional trainings to thousands of people both locally and across the Nation.

 **Deb Rauner, M.Ed.,** received a B.S. in Elementary and Special Education and a M. Ed. in Educational Psychology with endorsements in Elementary Education, Special Education (Mild/Moderate/Severe Disabilities and Behavior Disorders). Ms. Rauner has been a special education teacher for 33 years, with 17 years as a classroom teacher for students with autism, moderate and severe disabilities and 16 years as a Behavior Specialist.

Ms. Rauner has served students in self-contained classrooms and regular education classrooms and has also done consultation in early childhood classrooms, daycares, with home programming and at vocational sites. Ms. Rauner has provided a variety of training in areas such as Applied Behavior Analysis, Functional Behavior Assessment, Programming for students with Autism Spectrum Disorders, and Teaching Language and Designing ABA Classrooms using Verbal Behavior Strategies. Ms. Rauner is currently an Autism Consultant.

Made in the USA
Middletown, DE
29 September 2021